Contents at a Glance

ABSOLUTE
BEGINNER'S
GUIDE

(TO)

Winning
Presentations

Jerry Weissman with Bill Kaszubski

que

800 East 96th Street
Indianapolis, Indiana 46240

Absolute Beginner's Guide to Winning Presentations

International Standard Book Number: 0-7897-3121-5

Library of Congress Catalog Card Number: 2004100877

Printed in the United States of America

First Printing: April 2004

07 06 05 04   4 3 2 1

Trademarks

All terms mentioned in this book that are known to be trademarks or service marks have been appropriately capitalized. Que Publishing cannot attest to the accuracy of this information. Use of a term in this book should not be regarded as affecting the validity of any trademark or service mark.

Warning and Disclaimer

Every effort has been made to make this book as complete and as accurate as possible, but no warranty or fitness is implied. The information provided is on an "as is" basis. The authors and the publisher shall have neither liability nor responsibility to any person or entity with respect to any loss or damages arising from the information contained in this book.

Bulk Sales

Que Publishing offers excellent discounts on this book when ordered in quantity for bulk purchases or special sales. For more information, please contact

U.S. Corporate and Government Sales
1-800-382-3419
corpsales@pearsontechgroup.com

For sales outside of the United States, please contact

International Sales
1-317-428-3341
international@pearsontechgroup.com

Executive Editor
Candace Hall

Acquisitions Editor
Karen Whitehouse

Development Editors
Karen Whitehouse
Bill Kaszubski

Managing Editor
Charlotte Clapp

Project Editor
Matt Purcell

Production Editor
Megan Wade

Indexer
John Sleeva

Publishing Coordinator
Sharry Gregory

Interior Designer
Anne Jones

Cover Designer
Dan Armstrong

Page Layout
Bronkella Publishing
Michelle Mitchell

Table of Contents

About the Authors

Jerry Weissman is the world's number-one corporate presentations coach. His private client list reads like a who's who of the world's best companies, including the top brass at Yahoo!, Compaq, Intel, Intuit, Cisco Systems, Microsoft, and many others.

Bill Kaszubski lives in Los Angeles, where he writes about science, art, and technology.

We Want to Hear from You!

As the reader of this book, *you* are our most important critic and commentator. We value your opinion and want to know what we're doing right, what we could do better, what areas you'd like to see us publish in, and any other words of wisdom you're willing to pass our way.

As an executive editor for Que Publishing, I welcome your comments. You can email or write me directly to let me know what you did or didn't like about this book—as well as what we can do to make our books better.

Please note that I cannot help you with technical problems related to the topic of this book. We do have a User Services group, however, where I will forward specific technical questions related to the book.

When you write, please be sure to include this book's title and authors as well as your name, email address, and phone number. I will carefully review your comments and share them with the authors and editors who worked on the book.

Email: feedback@quepublishing.com

Mail: Candace Hall
Executive Editor
Que Publishing
800 East 96th Street
Indianapolis, IN 46240 USA

For more information about this book or another Que title, visit our Web site at www.quepublishing.com. Type the ISBN (excluding hyphens), or the title of a book in the Search field to find the page you're looking for.

The Wizard of Aaaahs

Once upon a time, I was living and working at the opposite end of California from Silicon Valley, in Hollywood. I had spent the first half of my professional life in the world of show business, as a television producer for CBS, as a freelance screenwriter, and as a sometime novelist. I helped create news documentaries, feature films, dramas, and musicals. I had the opportunity to work with some of the most creative minds in the industry, from the legendary Mike Wallace on down. If you know anything about show business, you know that it's filled with peaks and valleys, and I had more than my share of valleys. But I met many interesting people and learned a lot, particularly about the art of telling a story in a clear, convincing manner.

Then, in 1987, I had a conversation with an old friend, Ben Rosen, one of the top venture capitalists in the high-technology world, who was then chairman of the board of Compaq Computer Corporation. It was a conversation that changed my life.

Ben and I had met at Stanford University, where he was studying for his master's degree in electrical engineering and I for mine in speech and drama. The engineer and the artist met only because we happened to be competing for the affections of the same girl. Our interest in the girl quickly faded, but our friendship did not. Ben followed my subsequent career in television and was well aware of my interest in the art of communication. As Compaq's chairman, he was also aware of an issue facing the great computer company: Its CEO, a talented executive named Rod Canion, had never developed a comfortable and effective style for public presentations.

Ben called to offer me a challenge: "Rod has worked on his weakness as a presenter," he explained. "He's even been coached by some of the experts in the field. But it hasn't quite taken hold. Would you be interested in flying out to Houston to teach Rod what you know about communication?"

I was intrigued but a little reluctant. After all, I didn't know much about the world of business. But Ben closed the deal with an unusual offer: "Compaq has just come out with a line of hot, new laptop computers. I've seen that clunker you're still using." (I'd just laboriously drafted my second novel on Compaq's huge, old, "luggable" computer and had been coveting the sleek, new, expensive Compaq machines.) "Suppose we swap you one of our new laptops for your services?" he asked. I agreed on the spot.

I met with Canion at his Houston office, and Ben sat in on our session, watching as I taught Rod the basics of communicating a story with clarity and effectiveness. An hour into the program, we took a break, and Ben buttonholed me at the vending machine in the lounge. He was fascinated by what he'd seen. "Jerry," Ben said, with a snap of his fingers, "There's an enormous business opportunity here! I spend all day listening to presentations by CEOs who want me to invest in their businesses. You wouldn't believe how complex and dry most of them are. You ought to move up to Silicon Valley and teach these people some of your storytelling skills. God knows they need your help!"

> 66 I spend all day listening to presentations by CEOs who want me to invest in their businesses. You wouldn't believe how complex and dry most of them are. 99

Naturally, I was flattered. But I thought of myself as a television professional, not as a business consultant. "I don't know anything about Silicon Valley or the computer business!" I protested.

Ben pressed me. "That doesn't matter," he insisted. "I'll be able to introduce you to clients; I can show you how to run the business; I'll help in many ways."

Still I demurred, "It's not a good idea to do business with friends." Ben shook his head and dropped the matter, for the moment.

Like all successful people, Ben is successful because he is persistent, and he persisted with me. He talked about the idea, on and off, for six more months, but I was still hesitant. Finally, at Ben's insistence, I agreed to make a pilot trip to Silicon Valley to meet some of his associates. One of them was Andrea Cunningham, a woman who had parlayed her experience as public relations counsel to Steve Jobs at Apple Computer into her own successful national public relations agency, Citigate Cunningham, Inc.

When I got to Andy's office, she was in a fretful state over a presentation she was scheduled to make at a major technology conference. I took a quick look at a very rough outline she had prepared and suggested a simple reordering of her concepts into a more logical sequence. Then I skimmed through the high points of the new outline for her. Andy's frown gave way to a smile, and she said, "You're going to do very well here!"

My reluctance gradually melted away. I agreed to Ben's business proposition, and my consulting company Power Presentations was born.

> 66 I took a quick look at a very rough outline she had prepared and suggested a simple reordering of her concepts into a more logical sequence. 99

The Mission-Critical Presentation

In the first year of my startup, Ben, true to his word, introduced me to many influential people, primary among them were his venture capital colleagues, or VCs, as they are known in the trade. One of them was one of the most powerful men in Silicon Valley, Don Valentine. A founding partner of Sequoia Capital, one of the premier venture capital firms, Don had been one of the original investors in Apple Computer, Atari, Oracle, and Electronic Arts. Don granted me a courtesy interview, listened patiently as I described my services to him, and then said, "We have a company that's about to go public, and we think it'll do fairly well. It has a very esoteric technology that will be difficult to explain to investors. We're planning on pricing the offering in the $13.50 to $15.50 range, but if the IPO roadshow presentation is any good, we can probably increase that share price by a couple of bucks. I'm going to introduce you to the CEO and ask him to have you help him with his presentation."

The company was Cisco Systems. The CEO was John Morgridge. I helped John develop the presentation that explained the company's complex networking technology. The message got through to the investors. On the day Cisco went public, its stock opened at $18 a share and closed its first day of trading at $22 a share (a then-unheard-of price jump). Cisco quickly became the darling of the investment community and the media. In an interview with the *San Francisco Chronicle*, Don Valentine, speaking in his role as chairman of Cisco's board, "attributed 'at least $2 to $3' of the increase to Weissman's coaching. John Morgridge, president of Cisco, is somewhat less generous. He gives Weissman 'at least an eighth of a point' or 12 1/2 cents per share."

That was some 400 IPO roadshows ago. Among those others, I coached the IPO roadshows of corporate luminaries such as Intuit and Yahoo!. During that same time, I also helped another 400 firms, both public and pre-public, to grow their businesses.

Following the IPO, Cisco continued to call on me for their nuts-and-bolts presentations, ranging from prezos (as they are called inside Cisco) in their briefing centers given to small groups of potential new customers, to prezos in their annual NetWorkers conferences given to massive assemblages of end users. Then-Vice President of Corporate Marketing Cate Muther required that every product manager take my program. At the time, she said, "Jerry's methods of presentation are now part of our culture; they help prepare our managers for industry leadership." Today Cisco and many other high-technology companies continue to enlist my help in coaching their senior executives to communicate persuasively. The business press has called me everything from the man who "knows how to talk to money" (*Fast Company*) to "The Wizard of Aaahs" (*Forbes*).

The IPO roadshow is probably the most mission-critical presentation any businessperson will ever make. Succeeding in an IPO roadshow is the ultimate example of winning over the toughest crowd. The investors are both demanding and knowledgeable, the stakes are high, and a swing of $1 in the share price of the offering translates into millions. But if you extend the logic a bit further, every crowd you encounter in business can be your toughest crowd,

> 66 Every presentation is a stepping-stone on the path to ultimate success. 99

and every presentation you ever give is mission-critical. Every presentation is a stepping-stone on the path to ultimate success. If any one presentation fails, there might be no tomorrow. You never get a second chance to make a first impression.

Therefore, in my work with my clients, I treat every presentation as if it was as mission-critical as an IPO roadshow. I use this approach whether I am working to develop a private financing pitch, a product launch, a keynote speech, a panel appearance, an analysts' call, a shareholders' meeting, or a budget approval presentation. You can extend my array with your own presentation situations, be they external or internal, be they for an important contract, a major alliance, or a big sale.

Every business presentation has one common goal: the all-important art of persuasion, an art with literally dozens of applications for which everyone in business must be prepared. Persuasion is the classic challenge of sounding the clarion call to action, of getting your target audience to the experience known as Aha!

In a cartoon, Aha! would be represented by the image of a light bulb clicking on above your audience's heads. It's that satisfying moment of understanding and agreement that occurs when an idea from one person's mind has been successfully communicated into another's. This process is a mystery as old as language itself and almost as profound as love; the ability of humans, using only words and symbols, to understand one another and find common ground in an idea, a plan, a dream.

Maybe you've enjoyed moments like this in your past experiences as a presenter, speaker, salesperson, or communicator, moments when you saw the light bulb go on, as eyes made contact, smiles spread, and heads nodded. Aha! is the moment when you know your audience is ready to march to your beat.

I've written this book to share the persuasive techniques and tools I offer my clients. You can use them in your business on a daily basis. The presentation principles my clients have used to attract their billions of investor dollars can work for you, too.

> 66 Every business presentation has one common goal: the all-important art of persuasion. 99

In the following chapters, I show you how to discover the story at the heart of your presentation and how to structure and present it so your audience will care about it as much as you do. You'll discover how to create a presentation slideshow that will support you without stealing the show. And finally, we'll talk about ways to make sure that you create and sustain the interest of your audience when you're delivering your presentation.

> 66 The presentation principles my clients have used to attract their billions of investor dollars can work for you, too. 99

PART i

Your Point Is More Important Than PowerPoint

1

WHY PRESENT?

Don Valentine of Sequoia Capital, the legendary venture capitalist who introduced me to Cisco, sits through thousands of presentations every year, most of them made by shrewd entrepreneurs in search of funding for their new business concepts. Don is continually shocked by the failure of most of these presentations to communicate effectively and persuasively.

He once summed it up to me this way: "Jerry, the problem is that nobody knows how to tell a story. And what's worse, nobody knows that they don't know how to tell a story!"

Presenting Is Storytelling

This problem is multiplied and compounded 30 million times a day, a figure, which, according to recent estimates, is how many PowerPoint presentations are made every business day. Presentation audiences, from the Midas-like Don Valentines to overbooked executives sitting through run-of-the-mill staff meetings, are constantly and relentlessly besieged with torrents of excessive words and slides.

Why? Why wouldn't every presenter, seeking that clarion call to action, be, as the U.S. Army urges, all that they can be? The reason is that the overwhelming majority of business presentations merely serve to convey data, not to persuade.

When I moved from the world of television to the world of business, I saw immediately that those massive transmissions of information down one-way streets to passive audiences were not at all communication—with the emphasis on the *co*—they were one-way streets that grounded to a halt at a dead end.

In the television medium, ideas and images are also broadcast in one direction over the air, cable, or satellite; but there is a return loop, a feedback, an interaction that comes back barreling at the broadcaster in the form of ratings, critics, sponsors, letters, telephone calls, emails, and sometimes even regulatory legislation.

When the message of a television series is not clear, and when the satisfaction of the audience is not manifest, the foregone conclusion is sudden death: The series is cancelled. In business, when the point is not crystal clear and the benefit to the audience is not vividly evident, death may not be as sudden, but it happens nonetheless: The investment is declined, the sale is not made, the approval is not granted—the presentation fails.

In my Power Presentations programs for my clients, and in this book, I bring a media sensibility to the business community to deliver a set of prescriptive techniques and services that enables presenters like you to achieve their clarion call to action with their audiences, to get them to Aha!

A New Approach to Presentations

The techniques you'll learn in these pages are a blend of new and old concepts from a broad array of disciplines.

When creating television public affairs programs, I had to wade through hours of archival and new film footage and reels of videotape, rifle through massive reports, sort through stacks of interviews, and boil it all down to a clear 28-minute-and-40-second program that would capture—and hold—the audience's attention. I've distilled these story development methods into a simple set of techniques and forms for businesspeople like you. Most of the professional writers I've met use these same techniques to tap into the natural creative processes that every human being possesses.

In television, I worked in multimillion-dollar control rooms equipped with electronic character generators, vast color palettes, chroma key insertion, and computer-driven onscreen animation. These capabilities are now readily available in Microsoft's PowerPoint software, installed in over 250 million computers. Unfortunately, as I'm sure anyone who has seen a recent business presentation can attest, most presenters apply these powerful functions with all the subtlety of an MTV video. Instead, they should be following Ludwig Mies van der Rohe's advice: Less Is More. I've developed a simple set of guidelines to help you apply Mies's principle to create visual support for your presentations and help you design your numeric and text charts so that, rather than overwhelm, confuse, and distract your audience, they enhance and clarify your persuasive message.

In television, I directed both film and video cameras and then spliced and arranged their output into a compelling story. In doing so, I employed the professional practices of cinematography and editing to tell a story and create an impact on the audience. I've translated these sophisticated methodologies into a simple set of continuity techniques you can readily implement with PowerPoint to help you tell your story.

I've also drawn many of my communication and persuasion techniques from classical sources, such as the writings of Aristotle. (Please don't let the word *classical* intimidate you. A wise person once defined a *classic* simply as something that endures because it works. I predict you'll rediscover the truth of that definition in these pages.) In ancient times, rhetoric was considered the greatest of the liberal arts, and what the philosophers of old called *rhetoric* is, in fact, great storytelling. As you read, you'll come to see the relevance of Aristotle's concepts to all the types of stories you need to tell in business–storytelling that will persuade your audience to respond to your call to action.

Other methods I reference are based on established knowledge, as well as recent discoveries about the human mind. These scientific findings, which detail how all brains and eyes absorb information, relate directly to how every audience reacts to any data input.

This combination of traditional and advanced techniques for communication and persuasion offers what I'm confident you'll find to be a unique, and effective, system that will help you present to win.

> 66 What the philosophers of old called *rhetoric* is, in fact, great storytelling.... 99

You'll notice that I give frequent and significant emphasis to the word *story*, which is intentional. In this book, as in my programs and seminars, I focus first and foremost on helping you define the elements of your story and the story of your business. The traditional presentation skills are also important: body language, gestures, voice modulation, eye contact, and answering questions from the audience. But in this book, they take a backseat to defining your story.

> 66 Getting your story right is the critical factor in making your presentation powerful.... 99

This puzzles many people who've heard me described (inaccurately) as a "speech consultant," or even an "acting coach." In fact, some clients, when first meeting me say, "Oh, I don't need any help with my story. Just show me what to do with my hands while I speak. And show me how to keep myself from saying, 'Ummm.'" Fortunately for them, and for you, I won't honor that request in these pages. There are a couple of good reasons for this.

note

First, a plethora of other books is available in the marketplace that teach delivery skills, some reasonably well. Second, and more important, I'm convinced that getting your story right is the critical factor in making your presentation powerful—far more so than your delivery skills. In fact, I've found that, when the story is right, the delivery itself tends to fall into place, almost magically so. The reverse is never true. You might be the most polished speaker on earth, but if your story isn't clear and focused, your message will fail.

I'm interested in offering you advice that you won't find elsewhere. I will, however, provide you with a checklist for the physical presentation environment in the Appendix, "Tools of the Trade."

CASE STUDY: FROM UMMM TO AAAAH IN ONE DAY

In 1991, I got an anxious phone call from the public relations people at Microsoft, regular clients of mine. "We have a young executive here named Jeff Raikes," they explained. "He's scheduled to make a presentation about a new product of ours, and we wonder if you could help him prepare. It's called Windows for Pen Computers, the newest member of the Windows family of products."

continues

"Fine," I replied, "Let's book a three-day program for Jeff."

There was a slight pause on the other end of the line. "Well, we're very pressed for time. Jeff has only one day. But it's really important that his delivery skills get polished. He's very smart and knows his stuff, but he just isn't comfortable. Can you make a difference in one day's time?"

"I'll try," I said.

What happened next is revealing. As requested, I spent one day with Jeff. But I had no time to work on Jeff's voice or body language. Instead, we used our time to develop a cohesive vision of Windows for Pen Computing: what this remarkable new software product was designed to do, the markets Microsoft hoped to serve with it, the history behind its development, the benefits it offered computer users. In short, we created the story Jeff had to tell.

I helped Jeff make some decisions about his story: which elements were most relevant and compelling to his audience, which technical details were necessary, and which ones were superfluous. Then I helped Jeff organize his presentation so the key ideas would flow naturally from beginning to end. By the end of the day, we'd worked through the entire story. Jeff was not only in command of the material, but also comfortable about delivering it.

The results? Jeff's presentation went over phenomenally well. Afterward, the public relations people at Microsoft praised me for the job I'd done on Jeff's delivery skills, though in fact we'd never discussed those at all. Simply getting the story right helped to transform a hesitant and uncertain speaker into a dynamic and confident one. Today, Jeff Raikes is Group Vice President responsible for Microsoft's Productivity and Business Services and one of Microsoft's most prominent and effective spokesmen. Among his current responsibilities is Microsoft's Tablet PC, the evolved twenty-first-century version of the technology that began as Windows for Pen Computing.

The lesson: All the vocal pyrotechnics and animated body language in the world can't improve a confusing story, but a clear and concise story can give a presenter the clarity of mind to present with poise.

The Psychological Sell

I've described the classic art of persuasion as getting your audience to Aha! To be truly effective, however, one Aha! is not enough. The Power Presentation is a continuous series of end-to-end Ahas!

I liken making presentations to massage therapy. A good massage therapist never takes his hands off your body; a good presenter never lets go of the audience. The good presenter grabs their minds at the beginning of the presentation; navigates them through all the various parts, themes, and ideas, never letting go; and then deposits them at the call to action.

Notice the verbs I used in this analogy to describe the work of a skilled presenter: *grab, navigate*, and *deposit*. All three can be reduced to a least-common denominator verb: *manage*. People are the deciding factor in business decisions, and management is the number-one factor in investment decisions. The good presenter is one who effectively manages the minds of the audience. Therefore, the subliminal takeaway of the effective presentation is effective management.

> " Presenting, therefore, is essentially selling. "

Of course, no one is ever going to conclude explicitly that a good presenter is an effective manager, an excellent director, or a superb CEO. That's a bit of a stretch. But they won't hesitate to conclude the opposite. Unconsciously, the audience makes assumptions. If they are subjected to a presentation with a point that is unclear, they will be resistant to both the presenter and his call to action.

Influential investors such as Warren Buffett or Peter Lynch subscribe to the commonly held principle of investing only in businesses they understand. When your story is unclear, fragmented, or overly complex, the audience has to work hard to make sense of it. Eventually, this hard work begins to produce first resistance, then irritation, and then loss of confidence.

A recent book by Steve Krug about Web design has little to do with my business, but its title states my point succinctly: *Don't Make Me Think*. The effective presenter makes it easy for the audience to grasp ideas without having to work. The effective presentation story leads the audience to an irrefutable conclusion. The journey gives the audience a psychological comfort level that makes it easy for them to say, "Yes" to whatever the presenter is proposing. Presenting, therefore, is essentially selling.

Of course, I would never minimize the importance of having solid factual evidence that validates your business premise. A well-honed presentation is no substitute for a well-conceived business plan, just as a commanding speaking style is no substitute for personal integrity. You must have the steak, as well as the sizzle. Yet when two companies or two individuals of equal strength are competing, the winner is likely to be the one who tells the story more persuasively.

In the end, the most subtle impact of a clear and compelling presentation is perhaps the most powerful: The person who is able to tell an effective business story is perceived as being in command and deserving of confidence. When you are in command of your story, you are in command of the room. Your audience will follow where you lead—and so will money, influence, power, and success.

> " When you are in command of your story, you are in command of the room. Your audience will follow where you lead—and so will money, influence, power, and success. "

This is the core message and value of this book to you, no matter what role or level in business you currently occupy. Perhaps one day you'll go public with a company of your own, and then I hope the techniques you learn here will help you make millions. Before that happens, however, you have to get past many mission-critical hurdles because every business decision turns on your ability to tell your story. So, please use the same persuasive techniques you find in these pages in those scores of other stepping-stones along the way.

To help you master them, I'll show you how Cisco persuaded investors to provide billions in capital to support a technology so esoteric that, even today, few people really understand it. I'll show you how Yahoo! capitalized on the emerging fascination with the Internet by transforming an irreverent brand image into a meaningful investment presentation. And I'll show you how Luminous Networks, a telecommunications startup company, was able to raise $80 million in private capital during one of the steepest market declines in history. I helped create Power Presentations for each of these companies. I hope to do the same for you.

This book is about presentations, yes. But it's about much more than that. It's about psychology, about storytelling, about getting every audience to respond to your call to action. It's about presenting to win.

THE ABSOLUTE MINIMUM

- The problem with most business presentations is that they don't tell a story.
- Getting your story right is the critical factor in making your presentation powerful.

2

SO WHAT IS THE POINT?

The Problem with Presentations

Few human activities are done as often as presentations, and as poorly. One recent estimate has 30 million presentations made every day using Microsoft PowerPoint slides. I'm sure you've attended more than a few. How many of them were truly memorable, effective, and persuasive? Probably only a handful.

The vast majority of presentations fall prey to what I call the Five Cardinal Sins:

- **No clear point**—The audience leaves the presentation wondering what it was all about. How many times have you sat through an entire presentation and, at the end, said to yourself, "What was the point?"

- **No audience benefit**—The presentation fails to show how the audience can benefit from the information presented. How many times have you sat through a presentation and repeatedly said to yourself, "So what?"

- **No clear flow**—The sequence of ideas is so confusing that it leaves the audience behind, unable to follow. How many times have you sat through a presentation and, at some point, said to yourself, "Wait a minute! How did the presenter get there?"

- **Too detailed**—So many facts are presented, including facts that are overly technical or irrelevant, that the main point is obscured. How many times have you sat in on a presentation and, at some point, said to yourself, "What does that mean?"

- **Too long**—The audience loses focus and gets bored before the presentation ends. How many times in your entire professional career have you heard a presentation that was too short?

When presenters commit any of these sins, they are wasting time, energy, and the attention of their audience. What's more, they are thwarting their own objectives.

Each of these Five Cardinal Sins is quite separate and distinct from the others. Here's an analogy to illustrate: Suppose you and I were chatting and I said, "Let me tell you about what I had for dinner last night." My presentation would have a point, wouldn't it? You'd know what I intended to do, and I wouldn't be committing the first sin.

But why on earth would you care about what I had for dinner last night? Unless you had said, "Jerry, I'm bored with all the restaurants in the area. Can you recommend a new place?" Then, by telling you about the excellent meal I had at a hot new bistro last night, I would be providing a benefit to you, and I'd avoid the second sin.

Now, if I told you about my fine meal by starting with the dessert, then I went back to the salad, then jumped forward to the cheese course, then back to the main course, my story would have no flow. If, instead, I went from soup to nuts, it would have a clear and orderly path, and I'd eliminate the third sin.

If I described the courses I ate by using the phylum, class, order, genus, and species of every animal and vegetable product in the dinner, it would be far too technical and too detailed. If, instead, I confined my description to descriptive adjectives and simple nouns, I would avoid the fourth sin.

Finally, if I took four hours to tell you about a meal that took me only two hours to consume, my presentation would be too long. If instead I did it in five minutes, I'd escape the fifth sin.

> 66 The inevitable reaction of audiences to a Data Dump is not persuasion, but rather the horrific effect known as MEGO: Mine Eyes Glaze Over. 99

This analogy may be a little far-fetched, but the Five Cardinal Sins are all too real. And although each of the five is unique and independent of the others, they do have a least-common denominator, a Data Dump: an excessive, meaningless, shapeless outpouring of data without purpose or plan. The inevitable reaction of audiences to a Data Dump is not persuasion, but rather the horrific effect known as MEGO: Mine Eyes Glaze Over.

Why? Why would any presenter in her right mind do that to any audience? Would you do that if you were trying to attract potential clients? Would you do that if you were trying to clinch a sale, raise investment capital, or convince analysts that your company is solid? Hardly.

The objectives of all of the above presentations are varied, but they all have one factor in common. In every case, you are trying to get the audience to do your bidding, to respond to your call to action, whether that means endorsing a proposal, signing a contract, writing a check, or working harder and smarter. The Five Cardinal Sins stand in the way of achieving this goal.

The Power Presentation

Most people in business, including the most successful ones, are too busy living their stories to focus on telling them. They spend 12 or 14 hours every day working on competitive strategies, product launches, financial analyses, marketing plans, mergers and acquisitions, sales pitches—the plethora of vital business details that fill your days, too. They live, eat, sleep, breathe, dream, and inhale their businesses. They see every single one of the trees, but not the forest. They rarely have the opportunity, or feel the need, to take several long steps back from the details to visualize the whole and then describe it compellingly.

When a story-living businessperson has to sell the business story, the intense involvement in the minutia often proves a hindrance. She mistakenly thinks that for the audience to understand anything, they have to be told everything. That's like being asked the time and responding with complete instructions for building a clock.

The remedy is painfully apparent: Focus. Separate the wheat from the chaff. Give the audience only what they need to know.

> 66 Give the audience only what they need to know. 99

Persuasion: Getting from Point A to Point B

As social animals, we humans find ourselves called upon to persuade other humans almost every day. Persuasion is one of the crucial skills of life. The persuasive situations you face will be remarkably varied, each posing its own unique challenges and opportunities.

Yet all presentation situations have one element in common. Whether it's a formal presentation, speech, sales pitch, seminar, jury summation, or pep talk, every communication has as its goal to take the audience from where they are at the start of your presentation—Point A—and move them to your objective: Point B. The fuel for this movement is persuasion.

Recognizing this truth is the best starting point for learning the art of persuasion. It's fine if your presentation is entertaining, eloquent, or impressive. But that's not your main purpose in offering it. Your main and only purpose is to move people to Point B. That's the point! When the point is not apparent, you have committed one of the Five Cardinal Sins; when the point, Point B, is readily apparent, you have made your clarion call to action.

Let's take a closer look at what's involved in the challenge of moving an audience from Point A to Point B. In psychological terms, Point A is the inert place where your audience starts: uninformed, knowing little about you and your business; dubious and skeptical about your business, ready to question your claims; or, in the worst-case scenario, resistant and mentally committed to a position contrary to what you're asking them to do.

What you are asking them to do is Point B. The precise nature of Point B depends on the particular persuasive situation you face. To reach Point B, you need to move the uninformed audience to understand, the dubious audience to believe, and the resistant audience to act in a particular way. In fact, understand, believe, and act are not three separate goals, but three stages in reaching a single, cumulative, ultimate goal. After all, the audience will not act as you want them to act if they don't first understand your story and believe the message it conveys.

When I coach the executives of a company in preparation for their IPO roadshow, the audience for whom they're preparing will be composed of prospective investors. Point B is the moment at which those investors are willing to sell some of their holdings in Intel or Microsoft and invest those valuable assets in shares of the fledging company.

> 66 To reach Point B, you need to move the uninformed audience to understand, the dubious audience to believe, and the resistant audience to act in a particular way. 99

CASE STUDY: SELLING A TOASTER

Dan Warmenhoven, the CEO of Network Appliance at the time the company went public, began his IPO roadshow with this opening statement: "What's in a name? What's an appliance? A toaster is an appliance. It does one thing and one thing well: It toasts bread. Managing data on networks is complicated. Until now, data has been managed by devices that perform many tasks, and not all of them well. Our company makes a product called a file server. A file server does one thing and does it well: It manages data on networks."

If Dan had stopped his presentation right there, his investor audience would have understood what his company did. But they might not have bought its stock. So, I coached Dan to go beyond his description to add: "When you think of the explosive growth of data in networks, you can see that our file servers are positioned to be a vital part of that growth, and Network Appliance is positioned to grow as a company. We invite you to join us in that growth."

That last sentence is the call to action. Notice that Dan did not ask the investor audience to buy his stock. That would have been presumptuous and unnecessary; after all, their very job titles included the word invest. But the additional sentences gave Dan the opportunity to lead his audience from Point A to Point B. A synonym for *lead* is *manage*. The subliminal takeaway, again, is effective management.

Starting with the Objective in Sight

Point B, then, is the endgame of every presentation: its goal. The only sure way to create a successful presentation is to begin with the goal in mind.

This is an age-old concept. Aristotle called it *teleology*: the study of matters with their end or purpose in mind. Today's business gurus market the same idea. In author Stephen R. Covey's *The Seven Habits of Highly Effective People*, he stresses the importance of starting with the objective in sight—Aristotle in everyday garb.

Few executives study Aristotle these days, but Covey has been read by millions, to say nothing of the countless others who've heard about his ideas from friends and colleagues. Nonetheless, this crucial concept of starting with the goal in mind hasn't truly penetrated our thinking about presentations. Think of the many times when, after sitting through an entire presentation, you asked yourself, "What was the point?" (One of the Five Cardinal Sins.) The missing point is Point B: the call to action.

Unfortunately, and inexplicably, Point B is missing from all too many presentations.

> 66 The only sure way to create a successful presentation is to begin with the goal in mind. 99

If you're a sales professional, how can your customer reach the point of making a purchase unless you ask for the sale? If you're a corporate manager, how can the members of your team agree to support your new business initiative unless you tell them unmistakably what you need them to do and explicitly ask for their help? If you're an ambitious young worker, how can your manager give you the raise or promotion you desire unless you ask for it?

> 66 If you start your persuasive process with a clear focus on Point B, you have a far better chance of ending there, accompanied by your audience. 99

Obvious? Maybe. But it's surprisingly common for businesspeople to forget to focus on Point B when they communicate. If you start your persuasive process with a clear focus on Point B, you have a far better chance of ending there, accompanied by your audience. Ask for the order! Call your audience to action! Get to the point! Get to Point B!

Audience Advocacy

For the presenter to succeed in achieving the clarion call to action, the audience must be brought into equal focus with the presenter's objectives. To create that balance, I've coined the term *Audience Advocacy*. Mastering Audience Advocacy means learning to view yourself, your company, your story, and your presentation through the eyes of your audience.

In programs with my clients, I role-play potential investors, prospective customers, or would-be partners. In developing my own program material, I take the point of view of my clients. I urge you do the same in whatever presentation you are developing. Take your audience's point of view. This is a shift in thinking that requires both knowledge and practice.

Let me refer again to Aristotle, that pioneer in the art of persuasion. In his masterwork, the *Rhetoric*, Aristotle identified the key elements of persuasion, the most important of which he called, in the Greek of his day, *pathos*. *Pathos* refers to the persuader's ability to connect with the feelings, desires, wishes, fears, and passions of the audience. The English words we use today reveal connections with the ancient Greek root of pathos: Think of em*pathy* and sym*pathy*, for example. Aristotle wrote in *Rhetoric*: "...persuasion may come through the hearers when the speech stirs their emotions. Our judgments when we are pleased and friendly are not the same as when we are pained and hostile."

> 66 Everything you say and do in your presentation must serve the needs of your audience. 99

The question is: How can you communicate so your audience will be pleased, friendly, and ready to act on your Point B? My experience, and that of hundreds of my clients, suggests that the best method is Audience Advocacy. Everything you say and do in your presentation must serve the needs of your audience.

It's a simple concept, yet profoundly important. If Audience Advocacy guides your every decision in preparing your presentation, you'll be effective and persuasive.

Shift the Focus from Features to Benefits

One way to understand the concept of Audience Advocacy more fully is via one of the core concepts of advertising and sales: the distinction between features and benefits. This distinction is vitally important whenever you're called on to sell your story. In fact, when you shift the focus of any presentation from features to benefits you heighten the chances of winning converts to your cause.

A *feature* is a fact or quality about you or your company, the products you sell, or the idea you're advocating. By contrast, a *benefit* is how that fact or quality will help your audience. When you seek to persuade, it's never enough to present the features of what you're selling; every feature must always be translated into a benefit. Whereas a feature might be irrelevant to the needs or interests of your audience, a benefit, by definition, is always relevant. Without benefits, you have no Audience Advocacy. For people to act on anything, they must have a reason to act, and it must be their reason, not yours.

The same principle applies to any persuasive challenge you face. Features are of interest only to the persuader; benefits are of interest to the audience. Go with benefits every time.

Understand the Needs of Your Audience

You can create an effective presentation only if you know your audience: what they're interested in, what they care about, the problems they face, the biases they hold, the dreams they cherish. This means doing your homework. If you're in sales, for example, it's imperative that you take time to get to know your customers: how and why they could use your product, their financial constraints, their competitive issues, and how your product can help them achieve their personal or professional goals. And while you need to understand them as representatives of the marketplace or of a client company, you also need to understand them as human beings. What are their biggest headaches, fears, worries, aspirations, needs, loves, and hates? How can what you have to offer serve them?

> 66 Features are of interest only to the persuader; benefits are of interest to the audience. Go with benefits every time. 99

At times, your interests and those of your audience are bound to diverge, which creates the potential for conflict and frustration. You might dearly desire that raise, that lucrative sales contract, or that crucial loan or investment needed to keep your business afloat. Inevitably, your audience members will have their own motivations and issues that differ from your own. The art of persuasion is balanced by Audience Advocacy—in other words, convincing your audience that what you want will serve their interests, too.

CASE STUDY: CUSTOMERS ARE PEOPLE, TOO!

Alex Naqvi is the CEO of Luminous Networks, a private Silicon Valley company providing optical Ethernet solutions that enable the giant telecommunications carriers to deliver, on a single platform, a combination of Internet traffic, interactive and broadcast video, and voice services. Although a veteran in the industry, Alex usually finds the telecoms, as they are known in the trade, a crowd that is an especially tough sell. But, Alex has learned to recognize, understand, and respond to the interests and feelings of those audiences. Alex explains:

Our new technology makes it possible for telecoms to deliver better Internet service more economically than ever before. We thought that using Luminous Networks would be a no-brainer for any telecom manager.

Unfortunately, we weren't considering the point of view of our audience. I'm thinking of one potential customer in particular: a big, important telecom with a long history in the industry. Many of the managers we were hoping to sell our services to had been with the firm for 20 years. They were conservative and maybe a little afraid of the new and the unknown—both of which Luminous represented.

In our early days, we didn't understand how to reach out to an audience like that. We went in with a rather cocky attitude, talking about how our technology was "a radical paradigm shift for the new century." We described its advantages in a way that implied that anyone who didn't get it was probably kind of dumb.

Looking back, it's easy to see our mistake. We were alienating the very people we needed to win over. No wonder they didn't want to buy from us.

In time, we learned to soften our presentations. We started describing our technology not as a radical shift, but as a natural evolution from the current technology. We learned to send the message, "You're not dumb. The technology you now have in place was perfectly appropriate for its day. But now the world has changed, and Luminous is ready with the next-generation technology you and your customers need." As you can imagine, our sales results are a lot better with this approach!

It's funny: As engineers, we tend to look at the challenge of selling our story as a lifeless, logical proposition. We forget the human factor. The message must be honed to address those human motivations. We forget that it's living people we are selling to!

Getting Aha!s

Let's review what we've discussed so far.

When stories are complicated, when continuity is absent, when the audience is over-whelmed, and when the presenter doesn't establish a clear bond with the audience, presentations fail. The MEGO syndrome sets in. As a result, no business gets done: The investment isn't made, the deal isn't consummated, the sale doesn't happen.

Your goal, of course, is just the opposite: to get your audience to literally or figura-tively ask, "Where do I sign?" That is the essence of persuasion.

Persuasion is the art of moving your audience from Point A, a place of ignorance, indifference, or even hostility toward your goal—navigating them through an unbroken series of Aha!s—to Point B, a place where they will act as your investors, customers, partners, or advocates, ready to march to your drum.

It is only possible to move your audiences along this path when you follow the prin-ciples of Audience Advocacy: to place their needs at the heart of your presentation. The central expression of Audience Advocacy is presenting benefits rather than fea-tures.

Few communicators achieve the sheer exhilaration of end-to-end Aha!s. But most communicators can come a lot closer than they usually do—as you will when you apply the Power Presentations techniques in this book.

THE ABSOLUTE MINIMUM

- The only sure way to create a successful presentation is to begin with the goal in mind.
- Everything you say and do in your presentation must serve the needs of your audience.

3

YOU AND YOUR AUDIENCE

What's in It for You?

The key building block for Audience Advocacy, and a way to focus on benefits rather than features, is to constantly ask the key question: What's in it for you? It's based on the more common axiom, "What's in it for me?" I've shifted the ultimate word to *you* deliberately, to shift the focus from you to your audience. This shift emphasizes the ultimate need for all communicators to be focused outward, on the needs of their audience (*you*), rather than on their own needs (*me*). This is the essence of Audience Advocacy in action.

In referring to this key question, I'll use the acronym WIIFY (pronounced *whiffy*). By constantly seeking the WIIFY in any persuasive situation, you can ensure that your presentation stays focused on what matters most: getting your audience to move from Point A to Point B because you've given them a very good reason to make that move.

The WIIFY is the benefit to the specific audience in your persuasive situation. There will usually be one overarching, grand WIIFY that unites the entire presentation and is at the heart of your persuasive case.

For example, when an entrepreneurial CEO and her management team launch an IPO roadshow for potential investors, the WIIFY is, "If you invest in our company, you'll enjoy an excellent return on your money!"

> 66 By constantly seeking the WIIFY in any persuasive situation, you can ensure that your presentation stays focused on what matters most: getting your audience to move from Point A to Point B. 99

On the other hand, when a corporate headhunter makes a job offer to a sought-after young recruit, the WIIFY is, "If you join our firm, you'll be starting an incredible career with great pay, fascinating challenges, and the prospect of some day becoming the company president!"

When a partner in a marketing consulting firm makes a new-business proposal to the chief operating officer (COO) of a Fortune 500 company, the WIIFY might be, "If you hire us, the expertise we'll provide will improve your promotional plans, increase your market share, and boost your profits—and your personal stock options will double in value!"

WIIFY Triggers

In addition to these grand WIIFYs, there will usually be many smaller WIIFYs—more specific but still significant audience benefits that give meaning to each element in your presentation. In fact, every element in your presentation must be clearly linked to a WIIFY.

In my programs, I use six phrases I call *WIIFY triggers*. They're designed to remind presenters about the necessity of linking every element of their presentations to a clear audience benefit—in other words, a WIIFY. During the final run-throughs of presentations I've helped develop, whenever I hear an idea, fact, story, or detail without a clear audience benefit, I interrupt to call out one of these WIIFY triggers:

1. "This is important to you because...?" (The presenter fills in the blank.)
2. "What does this mean to you?" (The presenter explains.)
3. "Why am I telling you this?" (The presenter explains.)
4. "Who cares?" ("You should care, because....")
5. "So what?" ("Here's what....")
6. "And...?" ("Here's the WIIFY....")

Get to know these WIIFY triggers. Use them on yourself the next time you're preparing a presentation, as reminders to link every element to a WIIFY. (You might want to copy this checklist from the Appendix, "Tools of the Trade," and tack it on the wall for continual inspiration.) When you work on a presentation as part of a team, use these triggers on your colleagues and encourage them to return the favor. By the tenth time you pull a WIIFY trigger, you might catch a nasty look or two, but the quality of the resulting presentation will make it all worthwhile.

SIZE DOES MATTER

Jim Bixby was the CEO of Brooktree, a company that made and sold custom-designed integrated circuits used by electronics manufacturers. (It's now part of Conexant Systems, Inc.) In preparation for Brooktree's IPO, Jim rehearsed his roadshow with me. I role-played a money manager at Fidelity, considering whether our mutual fund might invest in Brooktree. During the product portion of Jim's presentation, he held up a large, thick manual and said, "This is our product catalog. No other company in the industry has as many products in its catalog as we do."

Jim set down the catalog and was about to move on to the next topic when I raised my hand and fired off a WIIFY trigger. "Time out!" I said. "You say you have the biggest product catalog. Why should I care about the size of your catalog?"

With barely a pause, Jim raised the catalog again and replied, "With this depth of product, we protect our revenue stream against cyclical variations."

The lights went on. This was an immensely important factor in the company's financial strength, yet one that could easily have passed unnoticed simply because Jim had forgotten to ask himself, "What's the WIIFY?" Always find and state your WIIFY!

In any presentation, before you make any statement about yourself, your company, your story, or the products or services you offer, stop and ask yourself, "What's the WIIFY? What benefit does this offer my listener?" If there is none, it's a detail that might be of interest to you and your colleagues (a feature), but one that has no significance to your audience. But if there is a benefit, be sure you explain it clearly, explicitly, and with emphasis, just as Jim did when I pulled the WIIFY trigger.

At this point, you may want to protest, "Wait a minute. My audiences aren't stupid. They can figure out the benefits of whatever I mention. They might even feel insulted if I spell it all out for them!"

This is not necessarily true. Remember the Five Cardinal Sins. One is lack of a clear benefit. An essential truth about Audience Advocacy is that most business people today are overloaded with information, with commitments, with responsibilities. When you make your presentation, you *may* have your audience's undivided attention...but not necessarily. Even if it takes them just a few seconds to connect the dots between the feature you describe and the implied benefit, by the time they catch up, you will have moved on to your next point, and they probably won't have time to absorb the benefit—or the next point. You'll have lost your audience, perhaps permanently.

By stating the WIIFY, you seize an opportunity. Although your audience members are eminently capable of realizing the WIIFY on their own, when you state it for them, you lead them toward a conclusion, which of course is your Point B. In doing this, you manage their minds, you persuade them, and you instill confidence in your story, your presentation, and yourself. Plus, you accomplish something else. The audience might have just gotten to the Aha! themselves, a moment before you stated the WIIFY. By articulating it, you win their agreement. They react with nods, thinking to themselves, "Of course! I've never heard it put so succinctly and clearly!" Effective management.

> 66 An essential truth about Audience Advocacy is that most business people today are overloaded with information, with commitments, with responsibilities. 99

This is a variation on the features/benefits distinction. When presenting to potential investors, a CEO may explain the best features of a leading product: "We've built a better mousetrap." But it's not the quality of the mousetrap in itself that the investors care about; it's the size of the market. The effective CEO presenter will then promptly move on to the benefit to investors: "…and the world is beating a path to our doorstep." When the WIIFY is right, everybody wins.

In fact, the power of the WIIFY even applies in our personal lives. Consider this example:

Debbie runs a small but growing catering business. In the past, she has managed to keep most of her weekends largely free of work, which her husband Rich thoroughly appreciates. Now, however, she has received the proverbial "offer she can't refuse": a request to cater a series of receptions at the local art museum that will keep her busy on weekends throughout the fall and winter. It will be quite lucrative as well as prestigious, but Debbie has to convince Rich to support her in this endeavor. Over dinner one evening, Debbie paints an eloquent word picture of how catering the receptions will put her company on the map, but she doesn't tell Rich how he'll benefit.

> 66 Although your audience members are eminently capable of realizing the WIIFY on their own, when you state it for them, you lead them toward a conclusion, which of course is your Point B. 99

To win Rich's support, Debbie should say something like this: "This contract could boost my profits from the catering business next year by over 50%. It'll be enough to let me hire an assistant manager who can run the business for three weeks next summer…while we take that European tour we've always dreamed about."

In this example, Debbie had to do more than simply reframe the idea to make the WIIFY clear. She also had to adjust her plans so that Rich will receive a definite personal benefit. One of the advantages of crafting a well-conceived WIIFY is that, if you haven't previously shaped your proposition to be a true win/win deal with benefits for everybody, presenting the WIIFY forces you to do just that. Improving your presentation can also help to improve the underlying substance.

There's an old adage: "You can never be too thin or too rich." I propose to amend that with: "…or offer too many WIIFYs."

note

One of the advantages of crafting a well-conceived WIIFY is that, if you haven't previously shaped your proposition to be a true win/win deal with benefits for everybody, presenting the WIIFY forces you to do just that.

The Danger of the Wrong "You"

One seemingly obvious aspect of the WIIFY principle that proves to be a stumbling block for many business people is the danger of the wrong *you*. Let me demonstrate:

One of my clients (I'll call him Mark) was the CEO of a company that manufactured dental instruments, wonderful tools of exceptional quality and precision to perform root canal procedures. Mark's prior experience had been as a top salesman for another dental instrument company. Now, as CEO, Mark was preparing to take his new company public. I was coaching him through a rehearsal of his IPO roadshow by role-playing, as I usually do, a high-powered fund manager at Fidelity.

Mark eloquently presented the strengths of his company, focusing in particular on the high quality of its products. As an example, he described the special features of the new dental instrument his company had developed. Mark held up the actual instrument, looked at me, and said, "With this instrument, you can do better root canal procedures, more quickly and with less pain."

I stopped him. "That's fine," I said. "But I'm an investor, remember? I don't do root canals!" He had the wrong *you*.

"Hmm," said Mark. He smiled, thought for a moment, and then held up the instrument again and said, "So, you can see that the tens of thousands of endodontists across this country and thousands more around the world who want to do better root canals need instruments like this one, and they'll have to buy them from us!"

Now that's the right *you*!

You can see Mark's problem: In trying to formulate the WIIFY, he'd lost sight of his audience, the *you* of the question, "What's in it for you?" Instead, he devised a WIIFY that referred to the ultimate end user of his product, the endodontists, to whom he'd previously been selling. To hone his appeal to the investors who were now his audience, it was necessary for Mark to carefully focus on their concerns, which related to the size of the market for his instruments.

Can you get away with the wrong you? Will your audience be able to translate the benefit to another party into terms that are meaningful to them? Of course, they can. But if they do, they will have to make a split-second interpolation to adjust to the correct you. During that interval, they might stop listening to you and start thinking.

Don't make them think! Consider those words a guideline for Audience Advocacy. Make it easy for your audience to follow, and your audience will.

Suppose the audience does make the leap themselves, translating the WIIFY into terms that are meaningful to them? In Mark's case, he would still be missing a golden opportunity to manage his audience toward Point B.

This problem of the wrong you is a surprisingly common one. Many of us in business have to sell ourselves and our stories to multiple constituencies, each with different biases, goals, preferences, interests, and needs. It's easy to lose sight of today's audience and address another's WIIFY.

FIGURE 3.1
The wrong *you*.

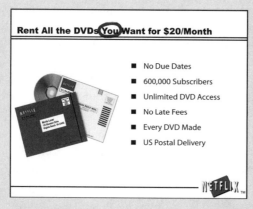

CASE STUDY: GETTING TO THE RIGHT YOU

Reed Hastings is the CEO of Netflix, an online DVD subscription company that went public in the spring of 2002. I worked with Reed in 1996, when he headed another company called Pure/Atria Software. At that time, I taught Reed, as I do all my clients, the subtle but important difference of addressing the correct you. Nonetheless, when Reed emailed me the draft of his roadshow for Netflix, one of the first slides in the presentation described his core business as shown in Figure 3.1.

continues

When Reed arrived for our coaching session, I assumed my usual role as a potential investor in Netflix's stock offering. I said, "Reed, this presentation makes me really eager to sign up and become a loyal subscriber of Netflix, but you didn't come here today to get me to subscribe. That can be handled by your sales force."

Reed smiled, and said, "What are you suggesting?"

On the computer, I made two changes and revised Reed's slide to read as it does in Figure 3.2.

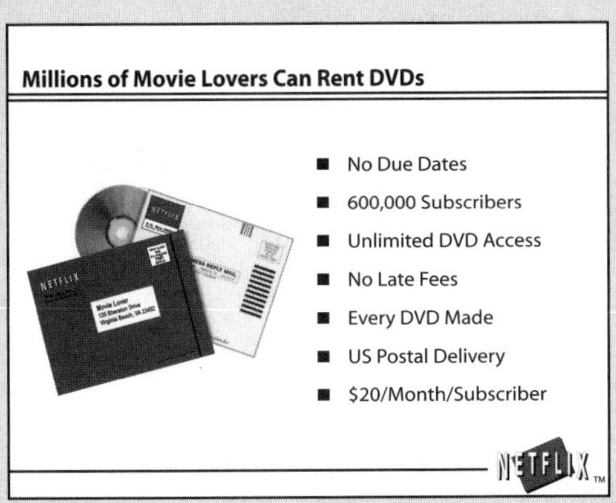

FIGURE 3.2

The right *you*.

Millions of Movie Lovers Can Rent DVDs

- No Due Dates
- 600,000 Subscribers
- Unlimited DVD Access
- No Late Fees
- Every DVD Made
- US Postal Delivery
- $20/Month/Subscriber

Suddenly, the entire frame of reference changed from the attractiveness of Netflix's consumer offering to how large the market opportunity was—a much more important consideration for Reed's investor audience.

Reed smiled broadly and said, "How about tens of millions of movie lovers?"

"Great!" I concurred. "How about, 'tens of millions…in the U.S. alone?'"

Reed accepted the revision, polished his presentation, and then left to begin his IPO roadshow. One month later, when Netflix went public, it offered 5.5 million shares for sale. It received orders for 50 million shares: oversubscribed by nearly ten times.

On their own, the members of the investor audience could have readily deduced that "All the DVDs You Want" really referred to the many millions of potential Netflix customers, but then the audience would have been doing the work for themselves. By providing the logic for them, Reed led them to a conclusion and, in doing so, built their confidence. Reed seized his opportunity.

Never take the *you* in the WIIFY for granted. You always need to give deliberate thought to who your audience is and what they want. If your WIIFY is designed for the wrong ears, it can fall flat.

The problem of the wrong *you* is a major reason to resist the temptation to create a generic presentation about yourself, your company, or your products. The generic presentation, or *company pitch* as it is frequently called, assumes that the same presentation can be used with few or no changes for a

> 66 You always need to give deliberate thought to who your audience is and what they want. If your WIIFY is designed for the wrong ears, it can fall flat. 99

variety of audiences. Wrong! The same story that excites and inspires your own employees might bore your customers and actually alienate and anger your suppliers, or vice versa. The same story that persuades technical customers to buy your product might confound your potential investors.

A perfect case in point comes from Alex Naqvi, the CEO of Luminous Networks, whom you met in the previous chapter. Luminous, which had started in 1998, planned to eventually go public, but given the challenging market conditions in 2001, Alex and his team decided to take their show on the private, rather than the public, road to seek additional financing.

Before we presented to the investors, we also did due diligence on them and their professional backgrounds. If they were from the technology industry or had worked for one of the carriers, I would tell the story differently; I'd use technology buzzwords that I knew they would understand. But if the investors had formerly been investment bankers, I'd explain our business differently. The key is that everyone in the audience should be able to relate to what I'm talking about.

We did a total of about 60 presentations. It was a very tough environment, a poor financial market. But in the end, the presentation helped us raise the money we needed—80 million dollars. When I tell people about it, they don't believe that we were able to achieve that given the tough climate we were operating in. But despite the climate, we did it because we found the right *you*.

THE ABSOLUTE MINIMUM

- The key to Audience Advocacy is to constantly answer the question, "What's in it for you?"

- If you constantly ask and answer that question, your presentation will be sure to address the needs of the people in the audience and, therefore, move them to action.

PART

CREATING YOUR STORY

IN THIS CHAPTER

- Techniques for connecting with your right brain and the plot of your story
- Brainstorming a presentation story with a group
- Figuring out what you've forgotten

4

FINDING YOUR STORY: CREATIVE BRAINSTORMING

As you've seen, a critical component of crafting a great presentation is that, first and foremost, you must get your story right. Although a strong speaking voice, appropriate gestures, and skilled answers to challenging questions are important factors, none of them will yield a really powerful presentation unless your story is clear and leads your audience directly where you want them to go: your Point B.

Creating your presentation begins with the development of your story. Here is one of the first places where traditional methods of creating a presentation can go wrong.

The Data Dump

Remember the MEGO syndrome? It strikes when Mine Eyes Glaze Over during a presentation that overflows with too many facts, all poured out without purpose, structure, or logic. When that happens, the presentation degenerates into a *data dump*—a shapeless outpouring of everything the presenter knows about the topic.

> 66 All too many business-people labor under the mistaken assumption that, for their audience to understand anything, they have to be told everything. 99

All too many businesspeople labor under the mistaken assumption that, for their audience to understand anything, they have to be told everything—to tell them the time, they have to be told how a clock is built. As a result, they give extensive presentations that amount to nothing more than data dumps: "Let's show them the statistics about the growth of the market. Then we've got the results of the last two customer satisfaction surveys. Throw in some excerpts from the press coverage we got after our product launch. Give them the highlights of our executive team's résumés. And don't forget the financial figures; the more, the better." I call this the Frankenstein approach: assembling disparate body parts.

The audiences to these data dumps are hapless victims. But sometimes the victims rebel. "And your point is?" and "So what?" are the all-too-common anguished interruptions of audiences besieged and overwhelmed by torrents of excessive words and slides. Those interruptions, however, are made more out of self-protection than rudeness. The fault, dear Brutus, is not in our stars, but in ourselves.

THE DATA DOESN'T TELL THE STORY, BUT YOU CAN'T TELL THE STORY WITHOUT THE DATA

I hope that you'll never inflict a data dump on any of your audiences. But performing one is vital to the success of any presentation. The secret: The data dump must be part of your preparation, not the presentation. Do it backstage, not in the show itself. (The Greek word *obscene* originally described any theatrical action, such as a murder, that was kept off-stage, out of the scene, because it was improper to display such behavior in public. In this sense, you can regard a data dump as literally obscene.)

What you need instead is a proven system to incorporate a thorough data dump into the development of your story. Brainstorming is the ticket. It's a process that encourages free association, creativity, randomness, and openness while helping you consider all the information that may (or may not) belong in your presentation. Later in the process, you can sort, select, eliminate, add, and organize these raw materials into a form that flows logically and compellingly from Point A to Point B. At the start, the key is not to apply logic to the materials, but simply to get them all out on the table where they can be examined, evaluated, and sorted. Do the distillation before the organization: Focus before flow.

Left Brain Versus Right Brain

Scientists have long been fascinated by the way in which different mental functions are centered in different areas of the human brain. Most of the higher brain activities occur in the cerebrum, which is divided into left and right hemispheres. According to most scientists, the left and right

> 66 Most presenters, when developing their stories, tend to apply a left-brain approach to what is really a right-brain process. 99

halves of the brain are responsible for different forms of reasoning. The left side controls logical functions. It's associated with structure, form, sequence, ranking, and order and tends to operate in a linear, first-one-thing-and-then-the-next fashion. The right side controls creative functions. It's associated with concepts and is essentially nonlinear in its operations. The right brain bounces around among concepts, following connections that are impossible to explain logically.

Building a presentation is a creative process. That means starting with the right brain.

Here's the problem: Most presenters, when developing their stories, tend to apply a left-brain approach to what is really a right-brain process. They try to jump immediately to a logical, structured, linear end product, when their right brain is still caroming around in nonlinear mode.

Why? Because businesspeople are essentially results-oriented rather than process-oriented. Now, I'm sure that you, like most businesspeople, are quite process-oriented when it comes to critical matters such as long-term strategy, product design, or problem-solving; but these are all subjects for offsite meetings. Backstage!

When it comes to results-oriented tasks, like a presentation to a very important client with a deadline (on-stage), you want to get there in the shortest distance between two points. A time-consuming process can delay the result. If the process (left-brain ordering) is not effective (a data dump) while the right brain is doing what it's going to do anyway (free-associate concepts), you will have to traverse that seemingly short distance over and over and over again. You'll end up spinning your wheels.

The solution is timing. It's not a matter of more time; it's about the proper use of time. Get the sequence right: Let the right brain complete its stream-of-consciousness cycle before applying the left brain's structure. Focus before flow.

> 66 Let the right brain complete its stream-of-consciousness cycle before applying the left brain's structure. Focus before flow. 99

The Speaker Is Out of His Right Mind

A vivid illustration of the distinct difference between right- and left-brain function-ing is spoken language. Speech reflects the way the right brain operates in its spon-taneity, its grammatical and syntactical messiness, and its frequent logical leaps.

Let me illustrate with an excerpt from the live presidential debate between then-Governor George W. Bush of Texas and then-Vice President Al Gore. The debate, in a town hall format, took place on October 17, 2000, and PBS anchor Jim Lehrer was the moderator. Each candidate was given a chance to respond separately to ques-tions posed by ordinary citizens. Here is Governor Bush's response to the following question: "How will your tax proposals affect me as a middle-class, 34-year-old sin-gle person with no dependents?"

I think also what you need to think about is not the immediate, but what about Medicare? You get a plan that will include prescription drugs, a plan that will give you options. Now, I hope people understand that Medicare today is—is—is important, but it doesn't keep up with the new medicines. If you're a Medicare person, on Medicare, you don't get the new procedures. You're stuck in a time warp, in many ways. So, it will be a modern Medicare system that trusts you to make a variety of options for you.

You're going to get tax relief under my plan. You're not going to be targeted in or targeted out. Everybody who pays taxes is going to get tax relief. If you take care of an elderly in your home, you're going to get the personal exemp-tion increased.

You're going to live in a peaceful world. It'll be a world of peace because we're going to have clearer—clear-sighted foreign policy based upon a strong military, and a mission that stands by our friends; a mission that doesn't try to be all things to all people. A judicious use of the military which will help keep the peace.

You'll be in world, hopefully, that's more educated, so it's less likely you'll be harmed in your neighborhood. See, an educated child is one much more likely to be hopeful and optimistic. You'll be in a world in which—fits into my philosophy; you know, the harder work—the harder you work, the more you can keep. It's the American way.

Government shouldn't be a heavy hand. That's what the federal government does to you. Should be a helping hand. And tax relief in the proposals I just described should be a good helping hand.

Remember (if you still can) that the original question had to do with how a 34-year-old single person with no dependents would be affected by the candidates' competing tax plans.

The response given by Governor Bush (soon, of course, to be President Bush) veers and rambles all over the place. He never specifically addresses the question of how a 34-year-old single person would be affected by his tax plan...except at the very end of his ramble with the broad, general assertion: "You're going to get tax relief under my plan," which doesn't explain how much relief or what kind.

Governor Bush begins by talking about offering an increased tax exemption to those who care for "an elderly," forgetting or ignoring the fact that the person who asked the original question specified that she had no dependents.

Next, he skips to Medicare (a subject of less-than-immediate interest to a 34-year-old). Then he skips further off the path on to the topics of world peace, military policy, education, and finally, work ethic.

Six subjects later, in his last sentence, probably recalling that the original question dealt with taxes, Governor Bush belatedly refers again to "tax relief in the proposals I just described," skimming over the fact that he never did describe any tax proposals.

Leaving the Left Brain Behind

I don't mean to pick on George W. Bush. Some of our most effective political leaders have been known to speak in a rambling, incoherent fashion (Dwight D. Eisenhower, for one). And, speaking crisply and logically is no guarantee of statesmanship or political wisdom. Depending on your own political views and personal tastes, you might find Bush's speaking style infuriating, comic, or refreshingly human.

My essential point is a more general one. An excerpt of spoken language, when transcribed and printed, will never read like well-crafted prose. As a personal example, I recently recorded myself during a program with my clients, delivering the same material I've delivered for nearly a decade and a half. When I read the transcription, I was most surprised to see how irregular my word patterns were. The reason: Spoken language is governed by the right brain. Rather than focusing on the rules of logic, grammar, syntax, and consistency, it flows freely, wherever the concepts lead.

> 66 Spoken language is governed by the right brain. Rather than focusing on the rules of logic, grammar, syntax, and consistency, it flows freely, wherever the concepts lead. 99

By contrast, the production of written language tends to be governed by the left brain. When most people sit down to write a letter, memo, or report, their minds are front-loaded with left-brain functions: logic, grammar, spelling, and punctuation. Rather than bouncing freely from one idea to the next, dragging in names, references, pronouns, and concepts that might or might not be clear, they move methodically through a sequence of points, meticulously self-correcting their syntax and logic as they go.

> 66 …because the writer ruled by the left brain is concentrating on the rules of logic, grammar, and so on, the natural flow of concepts is often impeded. 99

The result is a document that is technically correct. It doesn't contain fractured sentences like Governor Bush's, "You'll be in a world in which—fits into my philosophy; you know, the harder work—the harder you work the more you can keep," or repetitions like his, "Now, I hope people understand that Medicare today is—is—is important."

But because the writer ruled by the left brain is concentrating on the rules of logic, grammar, and so on, the natural flow of concepts is often impeded. Almost inevitably, the writer omits ideas that are necessary or includes ideas that are unnecessary, overly detailed, or irrelevant.

You've probably written documents this way yourself: sitting down cold at your keyboard and banging out a memo or letter, "editing" it for style and content on-the-fly, as you write. If so, you might have had the experience of reading the memo or letter afterward and discovering that you'd completely forgotten to mention an important fact or idea, or you might have stuck in a completely irrelevant detail. This is a natural by-product of left-brain dominance.

Starting the work of developing a presentation with left-brain considerations such as logic, sequence, grammar, and word choice (or, for that matter, the color, style, and design of slides) is simply not effective. Crafting a presentation is a creative task; it must start with the kind of creative resources that are available only on the right side of your brain. Use the right tool for the right job.

> 66 …start the story development process by doing what your brain is going to do anyway: Follow the stream of consciousness and capture the results during brainstorming. 99

Therefore, start the story development process by doing what your brain is going to do anyway: Follow the stream of consciousness and capture the results during brainstorming.

Managing the Brainstorm: The Framework Form

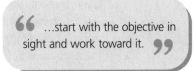

> ...start with the objective in sight and work toward it.

When you start to brainstorm about your very important presentation to your very important client, do you want to start by thinking about what you'll wear? I doubt it. Do you want to start by thinking about the rest of your schedule on the day of your important presentation? I don't think so. Attire and calendar are related to the presentation, but only peripherally. You needn't include them in your brainstorm.

Before you begin the brainstorming process, you must first tighten your focus past the peripheral. To do this, begin with the tool I call the Framework Form.

Think of your presentation as a blank canvas within a frame. This is where you will do your brainstorming. To tighten the focus, you need to set the outer limits, the parameters, of your presentation. They include the following elements.

Point B

Because most presentations lack a clear point (the first of the Five Cardinal Sins), why not start with it? In other words, start with the objective in sight and work toward it. Once again, this rule incorporates the wisdom of Aristotle and Stephen Covey.

Audience

Now that you appreciate the importance of Audience Advocacy, you must analyze what your intended audience knows and what they need to know to understand, believe, or act on what you're asking. Use the following three metrics to analyze your audience.

Identity

Who will be in the audience? What are their roles?

Knowledge Level

Remember that one of the Five Cardinal Sins is being too technical. You cannot be an effective audience advocate unless you know your audience and are prepared to communicate with them in language they understand. Therefore, it's important to spend time during your preparation process analyzing your audience and anticipating what they know and what they don't know.

> You cannot be an effective audience advocate unless you know your audience and are prepared to communicate with them in language they understand.

As a tool for assessing your audience's knowledge level, I've developed a simple chart, called the comprehension graph. It measures knowledge along the vertical axis, from zero (no background knowledge about the presentation topic at all) to the maximum (knowledge that usually only the presenter would have). The horizontal axis measures the number of people in the audience.

To use this graph, mark points along it that represent what fraction of your audience will be located at each knowledge level along the vertical axis. Thus, for a presentation about a new high-tech product to an audience that includes a large number of relatively unsophisticated listeners along with a handful of engineers and other knowledgeable experts, the graph might look like Figure 4.1.

FIGURE 4.1

The audience comprehension graph.

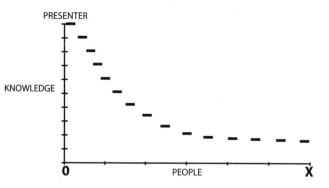

The specific shape of the line you draw should be constantly in your mind as you prepare and present your material. If only a few members of your audience share your level of technical or industry knowledge (as is often the case), you can't fly too high too long. You'll need to put significant effort into translating your technical information using language, examples, and analogies that everyone can understand.

When technical terms are unavoidable, you can raise the audience's knowledge level through the use of parenthetical expansion. Simply stop your forward progress and explain your complex concepts and terminology by parenthetically adding, "By that I mean…," and then going on to offer a clear and simple definition.

The WIIFY

"What's in it for you?" This is undoubtedly the most important factor in analyzing your audience. Remember that another of the Five Cardinal Sins is no clear benefit to the audience. Ask yourself: What does your audience want? How does the subject of your presentation offer it to them? How can you make the benefits to your audience crystal clear?

External Factors

These are conditions "out there," in the world, independent of you and your audience, which can impact your message and how it might be received. Some external factors will be positive, some negative. For instance, when making a pitch for investment dollars for your company, a rapidly expanding market for your product would be a positive external factor, whereas the emergence of powerful new competitors would be a negative external factor. You must consider all the external factors as you prepare your presentation. In some cases, you might need to change the content of your presentation or alter its structure to respond to unusually powerful factors.

> 66 You must consider all the external factors as you prepare your presentation. 99

Setting

Throughout the preparation process, keep in mind the physical setting for your presentation. These factors, too, can affect the content of your presentation. You can analyze the setting by asking and then answering these classic journalistic questions.

Who?

Will you be the only presenter? If not, how many others will be presenting before and after you? How will you distribute the parts of the story among the presenters?

When?

When will you be making the presentation? How much time will you be allotted? Will you have time for audience interaction? Will there be a question-and-answer period?

Where?

Will you be meeting in your company's offices, on your audience's turf, or in some neutral setting? How will the room be arranged? Will it be an intimate or massive setting? In a larger setting, where only you will have a microphone, it's likely you'll give the entire presentation uninterrupted. In a smaller setting, interruptions are inevitable. If so, allow time for discussion.

What?

What kind of audiovisual aids will you be using? Will you be doing a demonstration to show your product in action? If so, will there be room and visibility to perform the demo? When will you do the demo: before, during, or after the presentation?

A Form for the Framework

You need to ascertain all these factors and define them in writing before you start your brainstorming. Use the Framework Form shown in Figure 4.2 to assemble and capture all the previously mentioned information as you develop it.

FIGURE 4.2

The Framework Form worksheet.

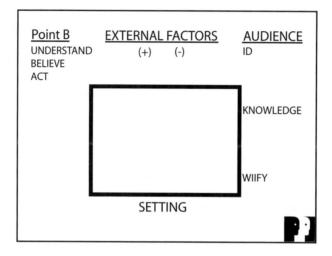

Define all these factors as clearly and as specifically as possible. There's no such thing as a one-size-fits-all presentation. The idea is to build a presentation tailored to one audience, on one occasion, presented by one set of presenters, conveying one story, with one purpose. A presentation that is less than custom-built will inevitably be less effective and less likely to persuade. Why bother with presenting at all if you are not prepared to invest the time needed to make your presentation all it can be?

Does that mean you need to start every presentation from scratch? Not necessarily. After you've done the process once, the second time will be much shorter, and shorter still for each succeeding iteration. In the nearly 15 years I've been in business, the process has never taken me more than an hour and a half the first time, regardless of the subject, from the most complex biotech company to the simplest retail story. It usually takes 15 minutes the second time, and less each time thereafter.

Eventually, you'll be able to click and drag parts of one presentation into another. The secret is to consider each presentation by starting with the basic concepts of the Framework Form. This initializing process will help ensure that your presentation, rather than becoming generic, is effectively focused on the specific persuasive situation you face.

> 66 There's no such thing as a one-size-fits-all presentation. 99

Resist any temptation to skip or short-circuit the Framework Form process. Don't take it for granted that everyone in your group knows and understands the mundane who-what-when-where-why details of your presentation. Lay out these facts in black and white; they will have a positive impact on what should and should not appear in your presentation, and in what form.

Now that you've set the context and focus, you're ready to begin developing potential concepts. Now your right brain output, instead of considering attire or schedule, can focus on more relevant ideas. You'll want to capture those ideas as they emerge, and that's where we turn to brainstorming.

Managing the Brainstorm: During the Session

Here's how to do productive brainstorming:

1. Set up a large whiteboard or an easel with a big pad of paper and lots of push pins to mount the sheets. I prefer a whiteboard because it allows me to erase and rewrite free-flowing ideas at will. It also results in a neater and easier-to-read set of brainstorming notes. Have on hand a supply of markers in several colors. Use different colors to indicate different groups or levels of ideas.

2. Gather your brainstorming team. It should include all those who will participate in the presentation as well as any others who have ideas or information to contribute.

3. You, as the presenter, or someone from your group (with reasonably neat handwriting), should handle the markers and capture the brainstorming ideas on the whiteboard. This person is your *scribe*. In my programs with my clients, I act as both scribe and facilitator. As a *facilitator*, I assume a neutral point of view and simply take down all ideas as they come up, without judgment. There are no bad ideas in brainstorming. Let them all flow. That is the essence of right-brain thinking. I also ask that each person in the group feed her ideas through me so as not to lose any ideas in side discussions, crosstalk, or digressions. I post all the ideas on the whiteboard for all to see and share. Have

tip

Several high-tech products on the market can capture written scrawls electronically from a whiteboard to a computer and then to a printer (my favorite is eBeam from Electronics for Imaging). These tools are very cool but not essential. You can always ask someone to hand-copy the notes during or after the brainstorming.

your scribe assume a similar role. Your scribe should not have a bias for or against any idea that emerges. Consider your scribe as Switzerland: neutral in all events.

4. Launch the brainstorming session by having someone, anyone, call out an idea about something that might go into the presentation. One person might say, "Management." You or your scribe should write the word *management* on the whiteboard and then draw a circle around it to turn that concept into a self-contained nugget.

5. As each concept comes up, the entire group should help to explode the concept. For example, after *management* appears on the whiteboard, pop out whatever ideas come to mind that are related to management. For example, there are the various members of your company's top management team: the CEO, the chairman, the CFO, the executive vice president. You or your scribe should jot these down as they come up, circle them, and link the circles to form a cluster of related ideas. Call the major idea in a cluster the *parent* and the subordinate ideas connected to it the *children*.

6. Continue to do the same for other concepts that people in the group suggest. Certain concepts come up in almost every business presentation: "our products," "our customers," "market trends," and "the competition." Depending on the specific purpose of your presentation and the issues your company is currently facing, some concepts are going to be unique to the presentation. As you work, you'll gradually fill the whiteboard with related concepts that might look something like Figure 4.3.

FIGURE 4.3

The results of the brainstorm.

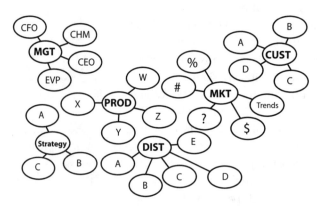

7. As you work, be flexible! Don't be afraid to bounce from concept to concept as necessary. While the group is exploding the concept of "marketing plan," someone might interject, "Oops! We forgot to list Jim, the marketing vice

president, as a member of the management team." No problem; squeeze Jim in on the whiteboard. If necessary, use the eraser. Someone else might say, "There's a market statistic I'd like to include, but I'm not sure the latest data is available." No problem; note the idea wherever it belongs with a question mark in the circle. The placeholder will remind you that further research is needed.

> 66 Avoid wordsmithing ideas. If you get bogged down in debating the proper words, you'll impede the free flow of fresh concepts. 99

As the brainstorming proceeds, you'll find that ideas pop up all over the place. The ideas will shift, connect, disconnect, and duplicate as they seek relationships with other ideas. This is your right brain at work. As ideas continue to come up, they will move around. Let it happen. Relationships will emerge, change, and develop. Capture all the activity on the whiteboard.

The Spirit of the Brainstorm

While your team is brainstorming, the right brain must rule. Remember that most businesspeople are left-brain-oriented, conditioned by education and experience to apply logic, reason, and rules to every activity. Learn to stifle this tendency during your brainstorming. Avoid wordsmithing ideas. If you get bogged down in debating the proper words, you'll impede the free flow of fresh concepts. It's hard to avoid wordsmithing at first, but you'll find it surprisingly liberating.

Remember: There are no bad ideas in brainstorming. Avoid censoring any ideas. The person whose idea is rejected is likely to feel rebuffed and might become reluctant to offer other ideas. When anyone mentions a new idea, jot it somewhere on the whiteboard, even if it strikes others as trivial or irrelevant. Even a needless idea can be useful because it can stimulate someone else to bring up a related fact that can turn out to be important. Get it all down. Don't worry about recording "too much" information; not everything on the whiteboard will end up in your presentation. Consider all ideas during brainstorming as candidates, not finalists. The right time to do the data dump is during your preparation!

Avoid thinking about structure, sequence, or hierarchy. If you find yourself wanting to say, "That idea ought to go up front," or "That idea ought to close the presentation," while other ideas are popping up, it would be like trying to rub your stomach and pat your head at the same time. Structuring front-loads your mind with sequence, order, and linear thinking, the hallmarks of your powerful left brain. Instead, let the concepts tumble out in nonlinear fashion, just the way the synapses of your brain fire naturally. Think about structure later. Remember: Focus before flow.

Give yourself enough time to do a thorough data dump. Don't put down your markers the first time there's a long pause in the conversation. Chances are the group is just taking a mental breather. Most brainstorming sessions feature two or three false finishes, each followed by an explosion of new ideas, before the group has really exhausted its store of information and ideas.

When you are truly done, your whiteboard will be filled with lots of circles. At that point, the entire group will be able to see all the elements of your story, all the candidate ideas, laid out for easy examination and organization in a panoramic view.

If any of this sounds familiar, it should: It is the kind of out-of-the-box thinking that many businesspeople use in strategic planning, product development, or problem-solving sessions. Well, these are the very same minds and the very same subject matter that go into a presentation. Why not use the same process?

One of the benefits of brainstorming is that it's like spreading out all the parts of a kid's bicycle onto the living room floor before you start trying to follow the all-too-complicated assembly directions or the way a chef lays out all the ingredients for a complicated dish before the cooking begins in what's called a *mise en place*. Spreading out the raw materials of your presentation gives you ready access to and control of all your ideas.

Contrast this approach with a left-brain, linear process. The typical left-brain method is to start by designing Slide 1: "Okay, we'll open with our company mission statement"; then Slide 2: "Now let's talk about the management team"; then Slide 3: "Now the statistics about the marketplace"; and so on. The problem is that, as you focus on the slides one by one, each slide effectively covers and hides the slide before. As a result, you're looking at only one concept at a time. You never see the whole story at once; therefore, you never see the best way to organize all its components into a single, compelling whole that flows powerfully from start to finish.

Instead, the brainstorming approach follows the right brain's natural functions. It allows your ideas to pour out in a random, nonlinear fashion, ensuring that every relevant concept (as well as every irrelevant one) gets a place on the radar screen. Later, you'll enlist the help of the left brain in bringing order to the raw materials you've generated.

Roman Columns: The Technique of Clustering

Brainstorming will generate a host of ideas of varying importance, loosely related to one another. The first step in getting from this relative chaos to an organized, clearly focused presentation is a technique known as *clustering*.

Actually, we've already used clustering to a degree. In the previous group brainstorming example, every time the group exploded a concept into a series of related concepts, forming a group of linked circles on the whiteboard, they created a cluster. These clusters reflected the natural relationships among the ideas as they poured out during brainstorming: parents and children.

Clustering is a necessary technique for organizing any complex material for presentation to an audience. It's also an ancient concept dating back to the classic rhetoricians of Greece and Rome.

Some Clustering Happened While Walking Around the Forum

There's a story, probably apocryphal, about a Roman orator whose memory was legendary. (It may have been Cicero, although the documentation is sparse.) The orator often spoke in the Roman Forum extemporaneously for hours, without referring to a single note. His secret was a memory technique that is still used today. We can imagine him explaining it to a curious admirer in a dialogue like this: "You asked me how I can speak coherently at length without written notes. Did you notice today how I walked around the Forum as I spoke?"

"Indeed I did. I assumed you did so in order to reach out to those in every corner of the audience."

"In part," replied the orator. "But there was a more important reason. As I walked from point to point around the edges of the Forum, I paused for a time at six different marble columns. Those columns are my memory aids. Each one symbolizes and reminds me of one group of ideas. Thus, rather than memorizing dozens of particular details, I have to recall only the six key ideas. Each of those key ideas evokes the details related to it."

Did Cicero really use this technique 2,000 years ago? No one knows for sure. But today I urge my clients to use the same technique in their presentations. Clustering lets you reduce the 40 or 50 ideas that fill your whiteboard to five or six Roman columns, the key ideas that will organize all the rest. Each column has a group of subordinate ideas. Now instead of trying to organize many ideas at the detail level, you can organize them at the 35,000-foot level.

Constructing Your Own Columns

When you look at your whiteboard filled with ideas, you will find key clusters emerging from the chaos. Examine the whiteboard and use a new colored marker to highlight the most significant ideas. The idea is to make the parents stand out visually from the mass of data, as in Figure 4.4.

FIGURE 4.4

Brainstorming results after clustering.

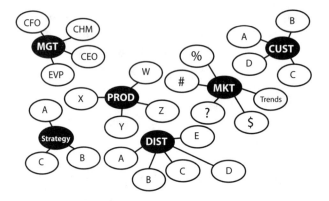

As your group works on identifying clusters, you might find yourselves identifying links and connections that didn't occur to you before. That's fine; just draw lines on the board as needed, or erase and redraw the circles if necessary. You might find yourself shifting concepts around: "Say, doesn't that point about the changing demographics of our market belong with 'key trends' rather than with 'sales potential'?" "How about connecting 'cost savings' to 'customer benefits' instead of to 'unique product features'?" No problem; move the children and link them to the most appropriate parent.

If some ideas seem to have no connection to any of your Roman columns, now is the time to ask whether those ideas are truly relevant and necessary. Perhaps they don't deserve to survive the transition to the finished presentation. And if you think of new ideas now that ought to be inserted, go ahead and add them. That's not at all unusual.

As you can see, the technique of clustering begins the process of organizing and introducing logic into the presentation. Having deliberately held back your left brain, you can now let it begin to get into the act.

Splat and Polish

You may be tempted to short-circuit the process by skipping the brainstorming stage. "Why not start with clusters of key ideas?" you might ask. "I could probably sit down right now and list the five main points we need to emphasize. That would save us all a lot of time." That's your logical left brain speaking. It wants to avoid the messy, uncontrolled process of free association. But the human mind doesn't work that way.

Start by unloading a "Splat!" of ideas in whatever order they came out, free form, a classic data dump. Organize them later, and later still polish them into words and sentences and paragraphs and, ultimately, into slides. I call this process *splat and polish*.

In my many years in the media, I've learned that this same process is followed by most professional writers, from novelists to journalists to playwrights to technical writers to historians. Not one of them will write a single page of text until they've done their research, brooded over their topic, and assembled a mass of notes about it. They might note their ideas on Post-Its, on dog-eared index cards, in spiral-bound notebooks, or simply in stacks of loose pages. Those notes, of course, are their data dumps.

Results-oriented businesspeople, unfortunately, don't use the same process when creating a presentation, or for that matter, when writing a report, speech, or memo. That's the way businesspeople are accustomed to think: Get to the endpoint as quickly as possible, Find the shortest distance between two points. They figure that the quickest way to get a presentation done is to just start writing. Logical, yes? Yes, and wrong.

CASE STUDY: WHAT DOES IT DO?

Here's a story that illustrates the pitfalls the splat-and-polish philosophy can help you avoid:

Judy Tarabini (now McNulty) was a vice president in the technology unit of the Hill and Knowlton Public Relations Agency when Ben Rosen, continuing his promise to help me grow my business, introduced me to the firm. After I delivered my program successfully to one of Judy's clients, she began to call on me regularly for her other clients.

In 1993, Judy joined the corporate communications department of Adobe Systems. It wasn't long before she called on me to work with Adobe. This time she had a high-level, mission-critical presentation: Adobe was about to introduce its Acrobat products and was planning to have its entire senior management team, about 15 strong, fan out into the market to make launch presentations. Judy was so positive about my program, she convinced Adobe's entire senior management team—including the founding chairman and CEO, John Warnock, and his co-founding partner and president, Chuck Geschke—to participate in a story development session with me.

As always, we started with a blank slate. I stepped up to the immaculate whiteboard in the amply appointed executive conference room at Adobe's then brand-new corporate headquarters in Mountain View. (They have since moved to even newer and more advanced facilities in San Jose.)

I started drawing out the executives. We began with Point B, we continued on to the WIIFY, and then we moved on to the brainstorming. As those very bright and very high-powered people spouted their thoughts, I raced to capture them on the whiteboard. We got lots of clusters: The Acrobat rollout schedule, the distribution plan, the Acrobat partners, the product benefits, the market, and many more. Before long, the whiteboard was filled to the edges with clusters of ideas.

continues

Then there was a pause. I looked around the room and said, "Please take a moment and look at all the clusters on the whiteboard. Tell me whether we need to alter any of the ideas, whether we need to consider shifting associations, or whether we've omitted anything."

A thoughtful silence ensued. Then suddenly, reverberating in the silence, there was a sharp thwack! Chuck Geschke had slapped his palm against his forehead, as in the "I shoulda' had a V-8!" television commercials. Then he broke into a sheepish grin and said, "We've left out what Acrobat *does*!"

Does that sound odd? Sure it does. But it happens a lot. You're so close to your business that it's easy to take key ideas for granted, to overlook or forget about concepts that are second nature to you but unfamiliar to your audience members. That's one huge process and rush past story development. Take the time to make certain that everything (and I mean everything) that might be relevant has had a chance to surface. Realizing what you omitted five minutes before the start of your presentation will be too late!

Focus *Before* Flow

Notice that so far, I've held off any discussion about selecting the sequence of ideas for your presentation, which is the left-brain process. First, get the heart of your story straight. Then, and only then, can you think about the most effective sequence of concepts for presenting that story persuasively. That's why, in my programs and in all my dealings with businesspeople, I repeat: "Focus *before* flow."

Now, having set the context with the Framework Form, having poured out all the concepts that might be relevant to your presentation by brainstorming (an efficient data dump), and having distilled those concepts and ideas by clustering, you're ready to develop the flow of ideas that will guide your presentation. That's the topic of the next chapter.

THE ABSOLUTE MINIMUM

- Start the story development process by doing what your brain is going to do anyway: Follow the stream of consciousness and capture the results during brainstorming.

- Clustering is a necessary technique for organizing any complex material for presentation to an audience.

5

PLOTTING YOUR STORY: FLOW STRUCTURES

So far, you've worked your way through the first three steps in creating an effective presentation. You developed the Framework Form, including your Point B, and you determined your audience's WIIFY and its knowledge level. You brainstormed potential ideas to include in the presentation and distilled those ideas into clusters, also known as Roman columns. You achieved right-brain focus.

Mapping Your Idea Forest

Now you're ready to shift to your left brain and put your clusters into a sequence to develop a logical flow. It's time to decide which Roman column goes first, which goes in the middle, and which goes last. In other words, you need a clear path that links all your Roman columns, a blueprint for determining the best order for the elements of your presentation. You need flow.

> 66 You need a clear path that links all your Roman columns, a blueprint for determining the best order for the elements of your presentation. 99

The best way to express the critical importance of flow to your audience is to start with the simple example of written text. One distinctive aspect of written text is that the reader has random access to the writer's content. If the reader, while browsing through a book, report, or magazine, encounters a word or reference that is unclear but looks familiar, the reader can simply place a finger in the current page and then riffle back through the prior pages to find the original definition or reference. The reader can navigate through the writer's ideas independently.

Your presentation audience does not have that capability. They have only linear access to your content, one slide at a time. It's like looking at a forest at the level of the trees, only one tree at a time.

You may be doing an excellent job of presenting one tree. Your audience might be suitably impressed, thinking, "That's a superb tree: deep roots, thick bark, rich foliage!" But if, when you move on to the next tree, you don't make it crystal clear how it relates to the first tree, your audience is forced to try to divine the relationship on its own. They no longer have access to the first tree, which forces them to work harder to remember it and draw the necessary connections.

At that point, your audience has three choices:

- They can fall prey to the MEGO syndrome.
- They can interrupt you to ask for an explanation.
- They can start thinking in an effort to understand the missing link, and stop listening.

None of these options is acceptable. Don't make them think!

Your job, therefore, is to become the navigator for your audience, to make the relationships among all the parts of your story clear for them. Make it easy for them to follow, to bring them up from the level of the trees and give them a view of the entire forest.

> 66 Your job, therefore, is to become the navigator for your audience, to make the relationships among all the parts of your story clear for them. 99

Doing this requires a roadmap, a plan, a formula. Like a chef who follows a recipe to use the right ingredients in the right order, you need to encompass all the Roman columns within an overarching template.

There are proven techniques for organizing ideas in a logical sequence to create a lucid and persuasive presentation. I call these techniques Flow Structures, and there are 16 options for various types of presentations.

The Sixteen Flow Structures

You can use these Flow Structures to group your clusters in a logical progression, making it easy for your audience to follow your presentation, as well as easy for you to construct your presentation. They are as follows:

1. **Modular**—A sequence of similar parts, units, or components in which the order of the units is interchangeable

2. **Chronological**—Organizes clusters of ideas along a timeline, reflecting events in the order in which they occurred or might occur

3. **Physical**—Organizes clusters of ideas according to their physical or geographic locations

4. **Spatial**—Organizes ideas conceptually, according to a physical metaphor or analogy, providing a spatial arrangement of your topics

5. **Problem/Solution**—Organizes the presentation around a problem and the solution offered by you or your company

6. **Issues/Actions**—Organizes the presentation around one or more issues and the actions you propose to address them

7. **Opportunity/Leverage**—Organizes the presentation around a business opportunity and the leverage you or your company will implement to take advantage of it

8. **Form/Function**—Organizes the presentation around a single central business concept, method, or technology, with multiple applications or functions emanating from that central core

9. **Features/Benefits**—Organizes the presentation around a series of your product or service features and the concrete benefits provided by those features

10. **Case Study**—A narrative recounting of how you or your company solved a particular problem or met the needs of a particular client, and in the telling, covers all the aspects of your business and its environment

11. **Argument/Fallacy**—Raises arguments against your own case and then rebuts them by pointing out the fallacies (or false beliefs) that underlie them

12. **Compare/Contrast**—Organizes the presentation around a series of comparisons that illustrate the differences between your company and other companies

13. **Matrix**—Uses a two-by-two or larger diagram to organize a complex set of concepts into an easy-to-digest, easy-to-follow, and easy-to-remember form

14. **Parallel Tracks**—Drills down into a series of related ideas, with an identical set of subsets for each idea

15. **Rhetorical Questions**—Asks, then answers, questions that are likely to be foremost in the minds of your audience

16. **Numerical**—Enumerates a series of loosely connected ideas, facts, or arguments

Let's look more closely at each of the 16 Flow Structures, with brief examples of each. The chances are excellent that one or more of these Flow Structures can serve you well in organizing virtually any presentation.

Modular

A presentation organized in modular form is a sequence of similar parts, units, or components in which the order of the units is interchangeable. Think of the Modular Flow Structure as a plug-and-play approach: The presenter makes an arbitrary decision about the sequence of units and then presents them to the audience, one by one. This is the most loosely organized of the 16 Flow Structures, which can make it challenging for your audience to follow.

Sometimes a presenter has no other choice than to use the Modular option. Financial presentations fall into this category; even a financial module within a larger presentation. In an IPO roadshow, the CEO usually uses one of the other, more accessible Flow Structures to organize the main components of the presentation in a meaningful order; but the CFO, who presents the annual results, quarterly results, balance sheet, income statement, and other financial data, can do them in almost any sequence. It hardly matters whether the annual results precede or follow the quarterly results. The CFO can simply order the items in whatever sequence feels right and discuss each one in order.

There are other instances in which the Modular option is appropriate. For example, it can be employed for a product introduction presentation that consists mainly of new product features.

> 66 Use the Modular option sparingly and preferably briefly. 99

The Modular Flow Structure provides a couple of advantages. If need be, you can easily rearrange the items at will. Or, if you're faced with time constraints, you can even omit one or two items. Convenient, yes, but challenging for your audience to follow and for you to deliver. Because there's no compelling logic to the clusters, everyone (that includes you and your audience) is under great pressure to try to track them. Therefore, use the Modular option sparingly and preferably briefly.

Chronological

Far more accessible than the Modular option is the Chronological Flow Structure, which organizes your clusters of ideas along a timeline. This option, reflecting events in the order in which they occurred or might occur, is ideally suited for any presentation where telling a story that deals with change is the most important objective.

You might have to make a presentation mainly to explain to the audience how a particular state of affairs came to be. For example, suppose you are the human resources director of a large company (let's call it Goliath Software, Inc.) that has just purchased a smaller competitor (David Software Co.). The announcement of the acquisition came as a surprise to nearly all the employees of both companies, and now many of them have questions and concerns: Why has this happened? How are the employees of these two companies, long-time rivals, supposed to begin working together? What do they have in common? What does the future hold?

Senior management has called a meeting to be held in the auditorium of David Software, the acquired firm, and you've been asked to make a presentation to "bring the new team up to speed." Point B, of course, is to help the David Software employees understand the acquisition and begin to feel as though they are a part of the new, expanded Goliath family of companies.

One effective way to organize your presentation could be the Chronological Flow Structure. Present a timeline showing where Goliath Software started, where it is today, how and why the acquisition occurred, and how the two companies will move forward together in the future. By making your audience conversant with Goliath's history and by showing them that the acquisition is a natural outgrowth of the convergence between the two firms, you are likely to assuage the concerns of the David Software team, and to begin to build strong connections with their new employer.

Physical

If the Chronological Flow Structure organizes your presentation according to the logic of time, the Physical option follows the logic of place. A presentation using a Physical Flow Structure takes its cues from geography, organizing clusters of ideas according to their physical locations.

Suppose your company is a distribution operation whose points of presence around the world represent its major competitive advantage. And suppose you are asked to make a presentation to an audience of potential customers who operate international businesses and are looking for a distribution partner who can serve their needs globally. You might organize your presentation according to the Physical Flow Structure.

You might introduce your clusters by saying, "Worldwide Distribution, Inc., has warehouses and shipping centers at 11 strategic locations on five continents, from the United States to Australia, from Brazil to France, from China to North Africa. To help you see why Worldwide is better positioned to serve you and your customers than any other distribution company, let me walk you through how each of those centers operates and connects within our global distribution network." This is an intuitive, easy-to-follow structure for the presentation.

Spatial

In contrast to the Physical option, which follows a literal geographic arrangement, the Spatial Flow Structure organizes your ideas conceptually, according to a physical metaphor or analogy, providing a spatial view of your topics: for example, from the top down, from the bottom up, from the center out, or from the outside in.

I often give presentations at industry or financial conferences, where I'm asked to discuss what it takes to create an effective presentation. For this purpose, I use a Spatial Flow Structure: from the bottom up. I depict this graphically as a pyramid, as in Figure 5.1.

FIGURE 5.1

The Spatial Flow Structure, applied to presentation skills.

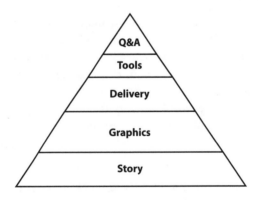

I make the point that every presentation has five primary components:

- Story development
- Graphics design

- Delivery skills
- Tools of the presentation trade
- Question-and-answer techniques

I go on to say that an effective presenter masters all five components. Of these five, the most fundamental is the story. I start with the story at the foundation and then go on to describe all the other components, working my way up the pyramid to the peak, the question-and-answer skills. As I go, I describe techniques to optimize each component, illustrating with examples and anecdotes.

The techniques and illustrations I use vary from one conference to another, but the Spatial Flow Structure remains the same. It creates an image that audiences find easy to understand, remember, and transmit to others: "What did Jerry say about the effective presentation?" "He said it's like a pyramid, with the story at the bottom and question-and-answer skills at the top."

CASE STUDY: FLOWING FROM THE BOTTOM UP AT INTEL

The Spatial Flow Structure can be used the other way as well: from the top down. Here's an example:

At Intel Corporation, Randy Steck and Dr. Robert Colwell were the leaders of an engineering team working in an atmosphere of the utmost secrecy to develop Intel's next-generation integrated circuit, the P6. (*The San Francisco Chronicle* wrote, "…you'd think the P6 was a tactical bomber rather than a computer chip." The episode recalled the title of the popular business book authored by Andy Grove, Intel's chairman of the board: *Only the Paranoid Survive*.) When Randy and Bob were ready to unveil the chip, they brought me in to help them and their team, including General Manager Dadi Perlmutter and Marketing Director Lew Paceley, to develop the launch presentation, which was to take place at the International Solid State Circuit Conference (ISSCC), a highly technical enclave of their peers.

The design team sequestered me in a hotel a short distance away from Intel's ultra-high-tech facility in Hillsboro, Oregon, where I led Bob, Randy, Lew, and Dadi through the steps I described in the previous chapters, including the Framework Form, brainstorming, and clustering, until we distilled all their ideas into the following clusters, or Roman columns:

- Design rationale for the P6
- P6 product specifications
- Potential end-user products
- System architecture and supporting chips

continues

The design rationale described the technology at its highest level (the concept behind the design); the product specifications described the result of the design; the potential end-user products described the applications of the P6; and the system architecture described how all the components worked together. Each layer drilled down a little deeper, from the top down, creating a Spatial Flow Structure.

After the presentation at the ISSCC, Bob Colwell wrote to me with a post-mortem:

I really felt sorry for the other presenters, who were incredibly nervous and did exactly as you predicted: classic data dumps on the audience.... Because I knew the presentation cold, I wasn't at all nervous when I actually took the stage, despite having the audience so big (about 1,800 people).... The Q&A period was interesting. I didn't get any of the hard-ball questions I was worried about.... I wonder if maybe potential hostile questioners were holding back, for fear of "losing" the argument to somebody who appeared to have done his homework and seemed thoroughly in control of the proceedings.

There are other uses of the Spatial option. For example, the market for a product can be presented in terms of concentric circles, like those on a target: The heart of the market, those customers who are most certain to be interested, are in the center circle (the bull's eye), while the outer circles represent other markets that are larger, more diffuse, and increasingly hard to reach. The center-out Spatial Flow Structure organizes these ideas in a way that's easy for an audience to grasp, follow, and recall.

The simplest variant of the Spatial Flow Structure is the physical metaphor of constructing a house. The foundation serves to describe the platform product or service; the supporting beams of the superstructure represent the organizations and partners; the wires and pipes of the internal infrastructure depict the technology; and the glass, brick, and mortar of the external interface stand for the marketing and branding. Many different companies in many different industries have tracked their entire business models with this recognizable format.

Problem/Solution

The Problem/Solution Flow Structure is attractive because it has a built-in WIIFY. When you use this option, you organize your presentation around a problem and the solution offered by you or your company. In this option, the benefit your company has to offer through its product or service follows naturally.

Many companies in the life sciences (pharmaceuticals, genetic research, medical devices, and health care) use this Flow Structure when doing a roadshow to raise private or public capital. To attract investors, they describe a particular medical problem and how they can solve it with their unique product or service. In their field, Problem/Solution is synonymous with illness/cure.

In the field of education, Problem/Solution is synonymous with learning. The essence of learning is to replace a lack of knowledge with skills. As a coach, I am also an educator, so I use Problem/Solution in my programs and in this book. Think back to the first chapter. It began with "The Problem with Presentations." Everything I've covered since then has been my set of solutions for you.

If you consider using Problem/Solution for your presentation, be careful about getting the emphasis right. Many people in business spend too much time on the problem and not enough time on the solution, leaving their audiences feeling as if they have slogged through a tragic Russian novel.

This matter of time and weight can best be illustrated with an analogy. In a Western film, the problem part (the Indian attack, the bad guys in the black hats, the tornado, the wildfire) lasts for a long time, virtually the full running length of the movie. That's because these problems produce suspense for the audience and empathy for the endangered protagonists. Those emotions are what keep the audiences glued to their seats, and buying lots of popcorn. The solution, by comparison, takes a very short time: the U.S. Cavalry arrives and rescues the hero and heroine. The End.

However, if you decide to use Problem/Solution for your business presentation, shift the weight. Touch on the problem very briefly and then bring in the Cavalry troops of your solution and let them parade majestically, in splendid full-dress regalia, complete with a rousing marching band. After all, that's the part of your presentation you want your audience to remember most.

Issues/Actions

Although virulent cancer and invasive surgery are clearly problems, remember this caveat about using the Problem/Solution option in areas of business other than life sciences: Businesspeople don't like to be reminded of their problems. Many sectors in the high-technology field, including software, hardware, and applications, court customers who are saddled with antiquated and cumbersome legacy computer systems. These customers are painfully aware that they have sunk a lot of time and money into equipment they can't simply abandon; they don't need salt rubbed in their wounds. So, rather than remind your audience about their problems, describe their issues and tell them what actions you and your company propose to address them. This is more than euphemism; it shifts from a negative focus to one that is concerned and active. Audience Advocacy in action.

The Issues/Actions Flow Structure is frequently used for presentations by companies that are in a turnaround mode. They identify the issues they are facing and the actions they are planning to take to overcome them, producing a list of clusters that might look like this:

> **Outline**—Turnaround Plan for Stumble & Falter, Inc.
>
> **Issue**—Out-of-Control Expenses

Action—Immediate Cost-Cutting Measures and Hiring Freeze

Issue—Unprofitable Product Lines

Action—Sale of Three Business Units

Issue—Flat Revenue Growth

Action—Accelerated Development of Two Promising New Products

Opportunity/Leverage

A close cousin of the Problem/Solution and Issues/Actions Flow Structures is the Opportunity/Leverage Flow Structure. With this option, you begin by describing an attractive business opportunity: a huge new market, a change in technology, an economic shift, or some other driving force. Then in the leverage section, you describe the superior products, distribution methods, partnerships, or competitive strategy your company has developed to take advantage of that opportunity. Again, this is more than euphemism or mere semantic difference. This structure directs the focus to your audience's interests and how you can meet them. It is the embodiment of Audience Advocacy.

The Opportunity/Leverage option is the Flow Structure of choice for most IPO roadshows because it appeals to the investor audience's essential interest in growth. Remember that I helped Cisco develop its roadshow presentation when it went public. At the time, Cisco's technology was an esoteric novelty. (Even today, as the established leader in computer networking equipment, its complex technology is still difficult for laypeople to understand.) Because the potential investor audiences for the initial offering did not yet fully understand how computer networks operated or why they would be so important in the future, the Cisco roadshow team decided to start its presentation by demonstrating the enormous potential of networking before trying to explain the technology that did the networking. Thus, the team chose the Opportunity/Leverage Flow Structure.

In the outline, the Cisco team began by describing the shift in computing from mainframes to PCs. This shift was neither a problem nor an issue; it was purely an opportunity. They then moved on to delineate the rapid growth of local area networks and wide area networks (LANs and WANs) and the recent improvements in technology that brought significant increases in speed, bandwidth, and power. They ended this cluster with a look at the anticipated shift in business from enterprise-centered to remote-based computing. All those trends, taken together, represented the opportunity.

Next, they talked about how Cisco's new device, called a *router*, could internetwork all networks. They explained how Cisco manufactured the router, serviced it, and sold it through channels and strategic relationships, and where Cisco intended to go with the router in the future. All these facts, taken together, represented Cisco's leverage of the opportunity.

Notice how this Flow Structure simplified and organized the presentation. Instead of having a dozen items for the presenter to explain and the audience to track, there were just two: opportunity and leverage. The forest view.

Form/Function

The previous three Flow Structures (Problem/Solution, Issues/Actions, and Opportunity/Leverage) are close cousins. The Form/Function Flow Structure is distinctly different. It moves your company's business offering (its solution, action, or leverage) into the starring role, front and center. Use it when you're presenting a single central business concept, method, or technology that has many applications or functions emanating from that central core. Think: one core technology and multiple applications; a main theme and several variations; a hub and its radiating spokes; a foundation idea and its dissemination by way of multiple franchises.

A salesperson might use the Form/Function option when presenting any product or service with multiple applications. For instance, the first salespeople who brought 3M's Post-It notes to market might have used this Flow Structure to introduce the novel lightly sticking glue (the form) and then gone on to describe its myriad uses (the functions).

The Form/Function approach is often used by biotech companies because it not only brings the franchise science to the forefront, but it also organizes complex subject matter.

Imagine that you're the CEO of Mom's Barbecued Chicken, seeking investment money to expand your business. In this case, Mom's barbecue recipe is the secret sauce, or the form. The functions would include all the ways the secret sauce could be developed as a business: by rolling out 600 franchised outlets, operating them with economies-of-scale, provisioning them with just-in-time deliveries, promoting them with co-op ads, and then by selling the secret sauce in 16-ounce jars in supermarkets and in plastic single-serving containers to airlines.

Make it once; sell it many times: Gillette's razors and blades, Kodak's cameras and film, HP's photocopiers and replacement toner cartridges. The cost is in the development of the core product; the profit is in the disposables—a high-profit-margin business. The form is the core product plus disposables design concept; the function is the way that design creates a high-profit-margin business.

SKINNING FORM AND FUNCTION AT BIOSURFACE TECHNOLOGY

BioSurface Technology went public on the strength of a novel tissue engineering technology it had developed. (BioSurface was later purchased by Genzyme.) The BioSurface approach was based on the fact that the human body tends to accept autologous (self) cells or tissue as grafts because it recognizes such tissue as its own. Conversely, the human body tends to reject allogeneic (non-self) cells or tissue because it recognizes such tissue as foreign and therefore rejects the graft. Patients with major burns don't have enough of their own skin to be used as grafts. BioSurface discovered a way to take a postage-stamp-size piece of a patient's skin and, in three weeks, grow it into enough autologous skin to cover the entire body surface.

In the BioSurface roadshow, CEO Dave Castaldi began by describing his company's innovative core science: how it extracted a patient's own cells, preserved them, cultured them, grew them, and then transplanted them back into a patient's own body without rejection. This core tissue engineering technology represented its form.

To demonstrate how it functioned, Dave then described how BioSurface was able to apply this science to a patient's own skin for permanent skin replacement, then to allogeneic skin from an unrelated donor for acceleration of wound-healing, then to cartilaginous tissue, and finally to ocular tissue. One form; multiple functions—and, of course, each function represented a potential source of revenue and profits for BioSurface and a business opportunity for potential investors.

Features/Benefits

This is the traditional product launch approach. In a presentation organized according to the Features/Benefits Flow Structure, you would discuss a series of features of your product, or your service, and for each one you would explain the concrete benefits provided to your customer. Once again, notice that the WIIFY is strongly woven into the very fabric of the presentation.

In the book business, each season's list of new book titles is presented by the publisher's sales representatives to buyers from the bookstore chains, such as Barnes & Noble, as well as to buyers from individual, independent bookstores. For each title, the representative is expected to explain the specific features of the book and the benefits it will provide to readers. A new atlas, for example, might boast features like larger type and brighter colors on its maps; the benefits to the readers are that the maps will be easier to read and use. The latest book in a series of thrillers might have as a feature "the most deadly and sinister conspiracy ever faced by Detective Cliveden"; the benefit is that the new book is a real page-turner. Fans of the series will spend several sleepless nights in delightful agony reading it.

If the sales rep presents a book's features and benefits convincingly, the WIIFY and Point B will follow naturally. The rep can say to the bookstore buyer, "As you can see, these features and benefits are sure to make this new book one that dozens of your customers will be eager to buy" (the WIIFY). "That means you'll want to buy a lot of copies to stack in the front window of your store!" (Point B).

Case Study

A case study is essentially a story, a narrative recounting of how you or your company solved a particular problem or how you or your company met the needs of a particular customer. In the telling, the case study covers all the aspects of your business and its environment. The Case Study Flow Structure provides a central spine that connects multiple diverse components.

We humans find stories, especially stories about people with whom we can identify, inherently interesting. Thus, a case study is an excellent way of capturing and keeping an audience's attention. It's an easy and practical way to make a product or service that is technically complex or apparently uninteresting become more vivid, personal, and understandable.

The human interest angle is particularly applicable in medical business presentations. Let's say your case study is about a patient named John Smith. You can describe the illness John has contracted, how many other John Smiths there are in the world, how much money is spent on all those John Smiths, and how long they've suffered without a cure. Then you can talk about how your company's drug cured John Smith, the patents you have on the drug, its regulatory status, its clinical status, the cost of manufacturing it, its average selling price, and its potential profit margin. Finally, you can describe how John Smith was rehabilitated and reimbursed, thus explaining how your drug will sell in the managed care environment. The story of John Smith provides a way to organize and humanize all the details of your company's entire story.

I helped develop the IPO roadshow of a company that digitizes television commercials and transmits and retransmits them, from the advertising agency to the broadcaster and from the broadcaster back to the agency, for audit. For the roadshow, we took one Dodge automobile commercial and followed it through the whole process, demonstrating all the company's services and products as a superior alternative to conventional shipping methods. The Dodge case study served as the spine for the entire presentation, making the company's capabilities—and its potential as a business—tangible and convincing.

Argument/Fallacy

Sometimes you must make a presentation in the face of a highly skeptical or even downright hostile audience. At such times, consider using the Argument/Fallacy Flow Structure, in which you raise arguments against your own case and then rebut them on the spot by pointing out the fallacies (or false beliefs) that underlie them. The idea is to preempt any objections in the minds of your audience, thereby creating a level playing field for a positive presentation of your company's real strengths.

This is a risky Flow Structure to use. It tends to sound either defensive or contentious and sets a negative tone. Reserve the use of this option for situations in which the negative ideas about you and your company are widespread and therefore unavoidable.

One company used this Flow Structure to its distinct advantage. The chairman of the board was scheduled to appear at a major investment conference to represent his company. He decided to title his presentation "Seven Reasons Why NOT to Invest in Us." He drew the seven reasons from negative analysts' reports, and one by one he rebutted them. When he was finished, the inescapable conclusion was that his company's stock was indeed a good buy.

Compare/Contrast

The point of the Compare/Contrast Flow Structure is to compare or contrast you or your company with others. How is your offering unlike that of any other company in your sector? How do you stack up against the competition? What is your competitive advantage? A presentation built according to this Flow Structure might focus on a series of comparisons, showing exactly what makes your company special along each parameter.

Like the Argument/Fallacy Flow Structure, choose this option with caution. By bringing another company into even partial focus, you run the risk of sounding defensive or, worse yet, having your audience remember the other company rather than your own. Moreover, when you attempt to throw a positive light on your own company by casting a negative light on another company, you can inadvertently offend someone in your audience who might have a direct connection with, or own shares in, the company you are criticizing.

For these reasons, save the Argument/Fallacy and Compare/Contrast Flow Structures for customer and industry presentations where you know your audience well and there's less of a chance that you'll generate negative feelings that don't already exist.

Matrix

You're familiar with matrices: those two-by-two, three-by-three, or four-by-four boxes that can be used to organize items according to combinations of ideas or qualities. Business audiences love matrices. Why? Maybe it's because a matrix imparts a quasi-scientific feeling, or maybe it's because, like many of the other Flow Structures, a Matrix Flow Structure organizes a complex set of concepts into an easy-to-understand, easy-to-follow, and easy-to-remember form.

The Matrix is a close cousin of the Spatial Flow Structure in that it organizes concepts in a visual format. The difference between the two is that the Spatial Structure implies dynamic relationships or movement (top-down, bottom-up), whereas the Matrix implies stationary or stable relationships.

Figure 5.2 is an example. It shows how the market for personal financial services might be divided into four categories, based on divisions along two dimensions.

FIGURE 5.2
A two-by-two matrix.

		NEED FOR FINANCIAL GUIDANCE	
		LOW	HIGH
INCOME	HIGH	Sector 1	Sector 2
	LOW	Sector 3	Sector 4

The two-by-two box creates a form you and the audience can follow through the whole presentation. You can analyze each of the four sectors in some detail, explaining why your company has chosen to focus on Sector 2 as the most promising sector in developing its business.

Parallel Tracks

The Parallel Tracks Flow Structure is a compound form of the Matrix option. It takes a matrix and drills down into each sector with identical subsets of information, or it takes a series of related ideas and drills down into each idea with an identical set of subsets.

Let me give you an example. This one is drawn from the world of biotechnology, which is one of the most technically complex of all subjects. Presenters need to work extra hard to find ways of simplifying and organizing their information. The Parallel Tracks option is one effective way of doing so.

Tanox, Inc., is a public biotechnology company that develops proprietary drugs to treat diseases that affect the human immune system, including asthma, allergies, AIDS, and others. For allergic diseases, Tanox's initial focus is to develop products that can treat asthma, seasonal allergic rhinitis (ragweed and pollen), and severe peanut allergy. The founder and CEO, Dr. Nancy Chang, a Ph.D. in biological chemistry, often has to present complicated scientific processes to an audience of investors, giving them sufficient detail to convey the business potential that Tanox's science creates.

Here is how Nancy uses the Parallel Tracks option: First, she talks about how, in allergic patients, their bodies produce specific Immunoglobulin E, known as IgE, to the specific allergens that the patients are allergic to and how IgE can trigger histamine release and cause all the disease symptoms of asthma and allergy. In Tanox's world, this is called the *allergic disease mechanism*. Then Nancy describes Xolair, Tanox's proprietary drug that treats allergic diseases. She describes how Xolair can potentially remove IgE from patients' bodies, thereby preventing the initiation of allergic disease and the resulting symptoms. In Tanox's world, this is called the *drug's mechanism of action*. Finally, she talks about the number of allergic patients who could potentially be treated by Xolair—in other words, the market.

Next, Nancy moves on to severe peanut allergy, AIDS, and others. One by one, she goes through each disease with the same points: the disease mechanism, the Tanox drug product and its mechanism of action, and the size of the market. By the time she finishes describing Tanox's product pipeline, her audience could almost sing along: disease mechanism, product, mechanism of action, and market. Thus, Parallel Tracks Flow Structure makes a set of complex and technical biological facts easy for a lay audience to digest.

Rhetorical Questions

This Flow Structure might be the ultimate form of Audience Advocacy. It takes the audience's point of view, immediately involving them by saying, "You might be wondering…" and then answering the question for them. Of course, it's best if the questions are ones your audience members are likely to have in their minds rather than ones you strain to devise. The use of the Rhetorical Questions option is not effective if the questions are forced.

An entire presentation could be built around the Rhetorical Questions Flow Structure. Each of your idea clusters could be linked to a particular question, which you would then answer.

Here's an example:

Cyrix, a company that designed, developed, and marketed semiconductors, went public in 1993. (Cyrix was later acquired by National Semiconductor and then by Via Technologies.) For the IPO roadshow, Cyrix CEO and cofounder Jerry Rogers decided to use the Rhetorical Questions Flow Structure.

In Jerry's opening statement, he said, "Cyrix competes against the established giants Intel and AMD (Advanced Micro Devices), as well as two other large, well-funded companies. So as a tiny startup trying to establish itself, I have to respond to some challenging questions from potential new customers about the IBM-compatible microprocessors that Cyrix designs. Three questions keep recurring: 'Will Cyrix microprocessors run all software applications?' 'How will Cyrix compete with Intel?' and 'Does Cyrix have the financial stability to succeed?'"

Jerry continued, "Cyrix has already begun shipments of the first commercially available 486 microprocessors not produced by Intel. But those same three questions about compatibility, competition, and finances remain important to potential investors like you. In my presentation today, I'll provide you the answers to those questions to demonstrate that Cyrix is indeed a sound investment."

Jerry showed the three questions on a slide. Then he spent a few moments and a few slides providing an answer to each question. His final slide showed three declarative sentences, answers to the three questions.

In the course of answering the three questions, Jerry covered diverse topics such as chip architecture, manufacturing strategy, average selling prices, intellectual property rights, the prospect of litigation, and the competitive landscape. But he tied all these topics together in three Roman columns and then tied the Roman columns together in the Rhetorical Questions Flow Structure.

Numerical

Finally, there's that old standby, the Numerical Flow Structure. "There are five reasons why our company represents an attractive investment opportunity." Then you list the five, counting down as you go. Like the Modular option, this is a very simple, rather loose Flow Structure. I recommend the numerical format only if none of the other options works for your presentation.

In 1983, Compaq Computer Corporation chose the numerical option for its IPO presentation. At the start of its two-week roadshow, the team offered 10 reasons an investor might want to buy shares of Compaq. But they soon found that all those reasons tended to drag on their investor audiences, with their occupationally short attention spans. The team quickly folded their 10 reasons into five and continued their roadshow to more attentive audiences.

The popularity of David Letterman's nightly "Top 10 List" brought the higher number back into favor. It also brought better luck for Hugh Martin, the CEO of ONI Systems, a provider of optical telecommunications equipment (now owned by Ciena Corporation), when he presented at the Robertson, Stephens and Company Technology Investment Conference.

I attended the ONI presentation and took a seat at the back of the room, as I always do at such conferences, so that I could watch the audience as well as the presenter. Most of the time, because few presenters provide flow (one of the Five Cardinal Sins), the MEGO syndrome quickly sets in. I see the backs of the audience's heads start to shift about. First, they glance down at their handhelds, then they lean over to whisper to their neighbor, then they look back to a copy of *The Wall Street Journal*, and often, before long, they jump up and leave the room to attend a different presentation.

Hugh Martin avoided that fate. He began his presentation by saying, "I'm a fan of David Letterman, and so, in the same spirit, I'm going to structure my presentation along the lines of the 'Top 10 Questions' I get from institutional investors." As Hugh stepped through the 10 questions, and his responses to each of them, none of those occupationally hyperactive heads shifted, and no one left the room.

After the conference, Hugh gave me the following post-mortem:

Robertson got enough positive feedback on that presentation that they are considering implementing the "Top 10" as a format. It really works because every investor wants to know what every other investor is asking. It also works for me, the presenter, because I don't have to worry about flow. There is a natural break between each "Top 10" question, which means I don't have to tee up the next slide in advance. Once I've introduced the question, it's easy to keep flow through the answer. Overall continuity is there because everyone knows you're simply counting down from 10 to 1. It's a wonderful format because it works for the audience and, truth be told, I can look really polished with little practice.

Selecting the Right Flow Structure

Is one Flow Structure better than another? Not really. Some structures work especially well in particular situations. Opportunity/Leverage generally works well for

investment presentations, and Form/Function generally works well for industry peer groups. But is
there a right or wrong way to organize any particular presentation? No. In fact, the 16 Flow Structures
overlap to some degree. The key is this: Choose one

> 66 Is one Flow Structure better
> than another? Not really. 99

or two Flow Structures for the entire presentation. Where presenters get into trouble is
when they choose all 16—sometimes all on each slide.

When you do make your choice, you'll elevate your audience from the trees to the forest. They'll be able to follow your presentation easily, and by navigating them through
the parts, you'll be sending them the subliminal message of effective management.

If you fail to choose, your presentation will drift, your audience will become confused
and drift too, and you'll never get them to Point B. It's less important *which* Flow
Structure you choose than *that* you make a choice.

Here's an example from the world of politics of how critically important it is to
choose and follow a Flow Structure. It's the State of the Union Address delivered by
President Bill Clinton in 1995 after losing his Congressional majority in the mid-term
elections:

1995 STATE OF THE UNION ADDRESS
- Change
- Status
- New Covenant
- Accomplishments
- New Proposals
- Balanced Budget
- Welfare Reform
- Crime
- National Service
- Illegal Aliens
- Tax Cut
- Minimum Wage
- Healthcare
- Foreign Relations
- Responsibility

Can you tell which Flow Structure President Clinton was using? Don't feel bad; no one else could, either. There was none. In trying to be all things to all people, Clinton's choppy address prompted David S. Broder of *The Washington Post*, one of the nation's senior political commentators, to write, "It was a speech about everything, and therefore about nothing." That is not exactly the kind of review you want to receive for one of your presentations. Broder and most others in the audience suffered from full-blown MEGO syndrome. Just to make matters worse, at 82 minutes, the speech set a record as the longest State of the Union Address.

> 66 It's less important *which* Flow Structure you choose than *that* you make a choice. 99

Apparently, President Clinton (or his speech-writing team) learned a lesson. The next year, this was the outline for his speech:

1996 STATE OF THE UNION ADDRESS
- Strengthen Families
- Education Goals
- Economic Security
- Fight Crime
- Clean Environment
- Lead Peace
- Challenge Washington

The President titled this speech "Seven Challenges," so the Flow Structure was that old warhorse, Numerical. Like all State of the Union Addresses, this was a complicated and lengthy speech, but the simplicity of the Flow Structure made it easy to follow. The audience—in this case, the nation—always knew where they were and where they were going.

Guidelines for Selecting a Flow Structure

When you are selecting a Flow Structure for your presentation, consider these factors.

The Presenter's Individual Style

Choose a Flow Structure that feels right. A little experimentation and practice will help you decide which option works best for you. The fact that one

> 66 Choose a Flow Structure that feels right...[and] that focuses on what interests or concerns your audience most. 99

of your colleagues had success with a particular Flow Structure doesn't mean that you will, too. Of course, this gives the lie to the very notion of the one-size-fits-all corporate pitch.

The Audience's Primary Interest

As you've seen, different Flow Structures emphasize different aspects of the story. Choose a Flow Structure that focuses on what interests or concerns your audience most. Remember that Opportunity/Leverage works well for investor presentations and Form/Function for industry peer groups.

A biotechnology company used the former Flow Structure for its IPO roadshow by starting with the opportunity (the market for its target disease) and then moving on to how its technology addressed or leveraged that market. Shortly after it went public, the company was invited to appear at an industry conference. For this presentation, it moved its form (that is, its technology, or its secret sauce) to the top and moved its function (that is, the market for its technology) to the later position.

Innate Story Factors

Some stories lend themselves naturally to a particular Flow Structure. Choose a Flow Structure that takes advantage of this innate organization. For example, a company or industry going through a transition is a prime candidate for the Chronological option.

The Established Agenda

If you are participating in a conference, seminar, or other gathering in which your presentation is expected to conform to a set format or respond to a particular challenge or question, use a Flow Structure that meets those requirements.

Esthetic Sense

This is another way of saying "instinct." If you have a strong feeling that one Flow Structure just "looks good" or "sounds good" or "works well" when applied to your story, then go for it! Don't try to cram your story into a Flow Structure that feels awkward. If you are comfortable making your presentation because it pleases your esthetic instincts, you will transmit your comfort to your audience and they will empathize with you.

As you can see, selecting a Flow Structure is more of an art than a science. You should also feel free to mix and match Flow Structures. It's quite possible to combine two or three Flow Structures in a single presentation. Try different Flow Structures, but don't limit yourself. The following case study shows how it's less important which Flow Structure you choose than that you make a choice—and stick to it.

A FLOW STRUCTURE WAS THE BEST MEDICINE FOR EPIMMUNE

Dr. Emile Loria was the CEO of a U.S. biotechnology company called Epimmune; its science was based on a naturally occurring substance called epitopes. Epimmune had harnessed epitopes to create vaccines to help the body's immune system fight cancer and infectious diseases.

FIGURE 5.3

Overview slide without a Flow Structure.

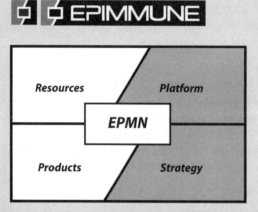

Emile asked me to review the Epimmune presentation he was scheduled to deliver at a biotechnology conference the following week. I received a copy of his presentation via email at home over a dial-up line, so it took about 15 minutes to download the image-rich file. I first looked at his overview slide (see Figure 5.3).

I called Emile and asked him which Flow Structure this represented. Although we had worked together many times, Emile hesitated. But then, after a moment, he said, "Aha! Form/Function!"

"Okay. Then why did you start with resources?" I asked.

After a moment, Emile exclaimed, "Of course! I should start with the Epimmune platform, our core science, our form, and then move on to how it functions with the products we derive from the platform, our strategy to develop the platform. And I should save the resources until the end to demonstrate how we will implement the strategy!"

FIGURE 5.4

Overview slide with a Flow Structure.

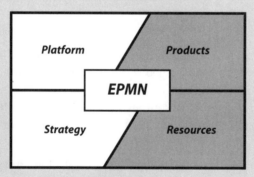

"Aha!" I concurred.

I spent less than 2 more minutes shuffling Emile's slides into the correct order (see Figure 5.4) and then tweaked a couple of other slides (very little tweaking was needed for this diligent student). Then I emailed the presentation back to Emile, which took another 15 minutes to upload.

Thirty minutes of transmission, two of validation. The forest view.

The Flow Structure approach provides an easy shorthand view of the logic and integrity of your ideas for both you and your audience. Your audience will be able to understand and follow any presentation. Even more important, they'll readily remember your ideas.

The Four Critical Questions

Let's review everything you've learned so far: Start with the Framework Form, do your brainstorming and clustering, and sequence them into a logical path with a specific Flow Structure.

All these steps can be further distilled into what I call the Four Critical Questions:

- What is your Point B?
- Who is your audience and what is their WIIFY?
- What are your Roman columns?
- Why have you put the Roman columns in a particular order? In other words, which Flow Structure have you chosen?

I begin every single program or seminar with every single one of my clients with these four questions. My advice to you, as it is to those clients, is to pose and answer each of these questions to every presentation you ever give from this moment on.

THE ABSOLUTE MINIMUM

- Your job is to become the navigator for your audience, to make the relationships among all the parts of your story clear for them.
- It's less important *which* Flow Structure you choose than *that* you make a choice.

6

STARTING YOUR STORY: CAPTURING YOUR AUDIENCE IMMEDIATELY

Picture your audience at the start of your presentation. Perhaps it's a group of potential customers who've come to hear you give a presentation about your company's newest product, drifting into a meeting room one by one, sipping their coffee, checking their handhelds. Or perhaps it's a banker in a wood-paneled office, sitting behind a tall stack of documents, probably loan applications, who must decide whether to lend your startup money for expansion. Or, as with my IPO clients, perhaps it's a roomful of institutional investors in an elegant hotel banquet room, wondering how the NASDAQ is doing while they're away from their offices.

What are they focused on? Chances are it's not you, not at the start of your presentation. Chances are it's on an urgent message on the handheld, the prior loan applicant, the mercurial NASDAQ, their next appointment, the report that's overdue, or the fight they just had with their spouse.

> 66 The Opening Gambit can overcome this problem. It's a short statement you use to seize the attention of your audience. 99

Why Are We Here Again?

If you were to launch into your presentation at full speed, describing your product, service, or technology, you would vault ahead of your audience and they would be hard-pressed to catch up. Don't make them think!

The Opening Gambit can overcome this problem. It's a short statement you use to seize the attention of your audience (and, simultaneously, to help you launch into your presentation in a comfortable, conversational manner).

In this chapter, you'll learn about seven proven options to consider in crafting your next Opening Gambit, with examples for each option.

Seven Classic Opening Gambits

- **Question**—A question directed at the members of the audience
- **Factoid**—A striking statistic or little-known fact
- **Retrospective/Prospective**—A look backward or forward
- **Anecdote**—A short human interest story
- **Quotation**—An endorsement about your business from a respected source
- **Aphorism**—A familiar saying
- **Analogy**—A comparison between two seemingly unrelated items that helps illuminate a complex, arcane, or obscure topic

The Question

One excellent way to open a presentation is with a question directed at the audience. A well-chosen, relevant question evokes an immediate response, involves the audience, breaks down barriers, and gets the audience thinking about how your message applies to them.

Scott Cook, the founding CEO of Intuit Software, used an Opening Gambit Question to powerful effect. Prior to Intuit's public offering, Scott appeared at the Robertson,

Stephens and Company Technology Investment Conference in San Francisco. Here's how he began his presentation:

> "Good morning, ladies and gentlemen. Let me begin today's presentation with a question. How many of you balance your checkbooks? May I see a show of hands?" Naturally, almost everybody's hand went up.

> "Okay. Now, how many of you like doing it?" Everybody's hand went down. There were chuckles in the room, and everyone was listening to Scott Cook.

> Scott continued, "You're not alone. Millions of people around the world hate balancing their checkbooks. We at Intuit have developed a simple, easy-to-use, inexpensive, new personal finance tool called Quicken."

It would have been deadly for Scott to launch into his presentation with a detailed description of Quicken; had he done so, his investment audience would likely have fallen prey to the MEGO syndrome. Instead, his Opening Gambit Question captured their interest and got them involved immediately.

But be careful with the call-for-a-show-of-hands question. It can be considered invasive. Many audiences have been there, done that, and won't appreciate being drawn out that directly. Besides, what if you don't get the show of hands you expect? The question backfires. Scott Cook pulled it off because he was a skilled presenter even before starting Intuit, having been a management consultant at Bain and Company.

An effective variation that avoids these dangers is to ask your audience a rhetorical question that is meaningful and relevant to them and then to promptly provide them with an answer. Mike Pope, who started as the CFO of DigitalThink, Inc., a public company that provides custom e-learning courseware, succeeded to the role of CEO. One of Mike's first jobs was to announce a new strategic focus for the company to the employees in an all-hands meeting. He was well aware that the new strategy, which involved belt-tightening, would have an impact on some of the employees' jobs. He chose an approach that emphasized the greater good for the company.

Mike began his presentation this way: "If I were to ask Fred here to define DigitalThink's strategic focus, he'd give me one answer. If I were to ask Lisa the same question, I'd get another answer. In fact, I'd probably get as many answers as there are people in the company. You'd all be right. That's because we're trying to be all things to all people. That won't work anymore. I'm here today to define our new strategic focus so that we can all be on the same sheet of music...and be successful as a company."

Mike then proceeded to lay out the new strategy. When he concluded his presentation, the audience

> 66 But be careful with the call-for-a-show-of-hands question. It can be considered invasive. 99

erupted in spontaneous applause and continued to buzz with positive feedback afterward. By offering them a plan that could produce better results (a WIIFY for them), Mike had prepared them to accept his new conditions.

The Factoid

An Opening Gambit Factoid is a simple, striking statistic or factual statement: a market growth figure or a detail about an economic, demographic, or social trend with which your audience might not be familiar. This factoid must be closely related to the main themes of your presentation and to your Point B. The more unusual, striking, and surprising your factoid, the better.

tip

The rhetorical question can be an excellent ice-breaker, as long as it's both provocative and relevant to your audience.

Adrian Slywotzky is a leading management writer and a vice president with Mercer Management Consulting. Adrian often speaks to groups of big-company executives to explain his views about the sources of business growth of the next decade and the strategies business leaders must use to tap those sources. To capture their attention, Adrian begins his presentations with a slide titled "The Growth Crisis." It lists several of America's biggest, most famous, and most admired companies from a broad range of industries.

Against this backdrop, Adrian says, "Every investor is looking for companies that can offer consistent double-digit growth in sales and profits. Of all the many great companies listed here, none can offer that kind of growth. Not one! It's startling, but true. Our research shows that once you subtract growth from company acquisitions and other special circumstances, none of these leading firms has been able to grow at double-digit rates over the past decade."

By the time Adrian has finished communicating this factoid to his audience (which is made up of executives at companies very much like those listed on the slide), many of them are feeling anxious, but all are ready to listen closely to Adrian's suggested solutions to the predicament.

The Retrospective/Prospective View

Think of this approach as "That was then, this is now." A retrospective (backward) or prospective (forward) look allows you to grab your audience's attention by moving them in one direction or

> 66 The more unusual, striking, and surprising your factoid, the better. 99

another away from their present, immediate concerns: that urgent message on the handheld, the mercurial NASDAQ, or that fight with their spouse.

For example, you could refer to the way things used to be done, the way they are done now, and the way you project them being done in the future. The contrast can highlight the value of your company's product or service offerings, thereby framing an effective lead-in to your presentation's main themes and your Point B.

A technology company can quickly capture the evolving power of its solution by showing the speed and capabilities of its products five years ago (a lifetime in the high-tech world), the vastly improved speed and capabilities of today, and the still greater speed and capabilities of the new line of products that will be going on sale in six months.

The Retrospective/Prospective approach can also be used to motivate. James Richardson became the chief marketing officer at Cisco, following a number of senior executive roles in his 13+ years with the company. He took on his new job at a difficult time. In 2002, the stock market had been battered, the tech industry in general was seeing slowed customer spending, and the telecommunications sector in particular was seeing reduced sales of networking equipment.

At the Cisco global sales meeting that year, the company's sales force was feeling hard-pressed to meet their quotas. James was a keynote speaker, and he began his presentation with a retrospective view that he quickly turned into a prospective view: "I've been where you are. I remember when it was no problem getting orders from our customers. It was easier then to capture opportunity when markets were growing very quickly. But the world is different today. That demand has greatly slowed. Now it's time for us to go out and seek new growth markets and new sources of revenue and start creating opportunity."

The Anecdote

By an Opening Gambit Anecdote, I do not mean a joke. I like a good joke as much as anyone, but my professional advice to you—and to every single person I coach—is never, ever tell a joke in a presentation. No one can predict its success or failure. Even if it does get a laugh, in most cases, it will distract from rather than enhance your persuasive message.

> 66 I like a good joke as much as anyone, but my professional advice to you—and to every single person I coach—is never, ever tell a joke in a presentation. 99

What I mean by an *anecdote* is a very short story, usually one with a human interest angle. Its effectiveness as an Opening Gambit lies in our natural tendency to be interested in and care about other people. An anecdote creates immediate identity and empathy with your audience. An anecdote is a simple and effective way to make an abstract or potentially boring subject come vividly to life.

Ronald Reagan, "The Great Communicator," never spoke for more than a couple of minutes without using an anecdote to personalize his subject. He was always ready with a brief tale about the brave soldier, the benevolent nurse, or the dignified grandfather as a way of illustrating his themes. Invariably, the tale would coax an empathic nod or a smile of recognition from his audience.

Newspapers and magazines regularly use anecdotes to capture their readers' attention. Just look at the front page of today's paper. You're sure to find at least one example of an Opening Gambit Anecdote. Every professional writer knows how well it works.

Here, from very different settings, are examples of how the anecdote can be used to launch a powerful business presentation.

In the spring of 1996, I worked with Tim Koogle, then CEO of Yahoo!, the Internet search engine company, as he and his team (including CFO Gary Valenzeula and founder Jerry Yang) planned its IPO roadshow. Tim and Gary would be the presenters, while the irrepressible Jerry would come along to answer questions. After considering several possible Opening Gambits, Tim decided to begin his presentation with a personal and true-to-life anecdote keyed to a concern he knew he shared with every member of his audience. His anecdote went something like this:

> Hello, ladies and gentlemen. As you can imagine, going public is a very busy time: There are SEC documents to file, meetings with lawyers and auditors, a roadshow presentation to prepare, and of course, a company to run. Imagine how I felt last week when I suddenly realized it was April and I hadn't prepared my tax returns. I had a host of questions about my return, and I hadn't even had a chance to sit down with my accountant.

> Fortunately, I work for Yahoo! So I logged on, clicked on the Yahoo! home page, clicked on the menu item called Finance, then clicked on the menu item called Taxes...and the answers to all my questions were right there.

> When you consider that Yahoo! provides this kind of powerful Internet search service for a vast array of subjects, from finance to travel to entertainment to sports to health, and then consider the growing legions of users of the Internet, you'll see that the advertising revenues Yahoo! can derive from those legions of users represents a very attractive business opportunity. We invite you to join us.

The Yahoo! IPO story has an interesting extra twist that sheds light on some other presentation principles. A key element of the Yahoo! business model was to promote its brand with a youthful, irreverent, and upbeat image, expressed by its name, its advertising, and even by the cartoon-like letters of its bright yellow and purple logo. In planning the IPO roadshow, the Yahoo! team and its advisors pondered ways to capture that brash image without alienating staid investors. At one point, they even considered wearing satin team jackets in the company colors for the roadshow and distributing bright yellow kazoos emblazoned with the company logo. These plans were abandoned in favor of a short video intended to set the tone at the very beginning of the presentation. Shot in MTV fashion, replete with fast cuts and odd camera angles, the clip featured exuberant youngsters running, jumping, and performing antics while shouting, "Do you Yahoo!?"

By all standards, the video was very well done. And as a television veteran, you might have assumed that I'd have welcomed the idea of starting a presentation with a video clip. But as I always do when a video is considered, I recommended that it be relegated to second position, after Tim Koogle's Opening Gambit Anecdote. After all, I reasoned, the primary investment consideration was management, not slick videos. In fact, Tim had been recruited to run the upstart company because he had gravitas. He had served as the president of Intermec Corporation, a division of Litton Industries, and prior to that, had spent eight years at Motorola. Tim's history of success in these respected, "grown-up" businesses would go a long way toward getting the investment community to take the Yahoo! kids seriously. Why not make management the star?

The investment bankers underwriting Yahoo!'s IPO overruled my recommendation. It was probably one of the few times in history that the advice of a media person was rejected by an investment banker as being too conservative. The video ran first. In the end, it didn't matter much. Yahoo! was so hot that its bandwagon rolled merrily along, with legions of eager riders clamoring to get onboard.

Three years earlier, however, in a similar situation, my counsel was heeded. Macromedia, a company that makes software authoring tools for multimedia, engaged me to coach their IPO roadshow team. I didn't get around to starting my program with them until after they had used in-house resources to develop an animated film to open their roadshow. The film clip, in which a sparkling, animated, golden *M* danced onto the screen while performing spins and leaps to effervescent soundtrack music, was quite impressive. Nevertheless, as always, I recommended that the film be relegated to second position, after the CEO's Opening Gambit.

Then I helped Macromedia CEO Bud Colligan develop the following anecdote:

> Good afternoon, ladies and gentlemen. Welcome to the Macromedia public offering. Last year, I was king of the hill at Apple Computer. I had a great job that provided me with boundless resources, deep staff, and abundant budgets. Why, you might ask, would I make the leap to this risky startup? The reason is that my job at Apple was to evaluate and develop new technologies. A lot of fascinating new programs and devices came across my desk, but the one that really caught my eye was multimedia.

> Now I'm sure that you've all heard a lot about multimedia lately. The word seems to be on everybody's lips. But if you were to ask someone to explain the term, most people would have trouble doing so. So, rather than try to define multimedia, let me show you multimedia.

Then Bud ran the film clip. Thanks to Bud's Opening Gambit Anecdote, the film was much more than a charming bit of fluff. It was also an impressive demonstration of the kind of creativity Macromedia could make available to millions of customers and therefore was highly relevant to Macromedia's Point B.

Now, let's consider an example from a completely different business setting: Argus Insurance is a Yakima, Washington-based company that sells worksite insurance benefit plans to company employees. These are customized plans that allow each employee to pick the types of coverage he most needs and wants to pay for, above and beyond the insurance provided by his employer.

Traditionally, Argus agents had simply visited companies, gathered employees in a room, and showed them a generic videotape about its service. The Argus agents then handed out pamphlets and waited to take orders, which were too often few and far between.

When I worked with a group from Argus, I introduced them to the concept of the Opening Gambit. With just a little help, Carol Case, an Argus Insurance agent, came up with the following Opening Gambit based on a real-life scenario:

> Last year, one of Argus's customers had a fire in her home. They think an electrical short might have caused it, but no one really knows. Anyway, the home burned down, destroying almost everything she owned. Talk about a disaster! Not only did she lose her home, she was financially crippled as well.

> Our insured, like many people, now realizes she could be just one step away from disaster. Luckily, we at Argus Insurance had a solution. Argus reviewed her previous insurance plan and found gaps in the coverage. We then provided quotes for comprehensive, low-cost insurance that provided coverage not provided by her previous policy.

Any human being can identify with this scenario. Carol is signing up many more Argus customers now than in the past, thanks largely to the power of a compelling Opening Gambit.

> 66 Please resist the temptation to go down to your local bookstore or library and get one of those *Ten Million Quotations for All Occasions* books. 99

The Quotation

Another option is the Opening Gambit Quotation. I don't mean a quotation from William Shakespeare, Winston Churchill, John F. Kennedy, or even Tom Peters...unless one of them specifically said something about your company. But if you can provide an endorsement or positive comment about you, your products, or your services from *The Wall Street Journal* or the industry press, the quotation provides relevant value. An endorsing quotation can capture your audience's interest and give you credibility at the outset of your presentation.

Please resist the temptation to go down to your local bookstore or library and get one of those *Ten Million Quotations for All Occasions* books. Most often, all those quotations turn out to be inappropriate for any occasion.

When DigitalThink went public in 1999, Mike Pope was the CFO. At the time, the Internet was bubbling into high froth and a host of other companies in the e-learning space were going public, too. Three years later, upon Mike's succession to CEO, I delivered my Power Presentations program to him, and I noticed that Mike smiled knowingly when I introduced the Opening Gambit Quotation option.

Why the smile? Mike explained, "The year we went public, almost every e-learning IPO roadshow used a quotation from John Chambers [the CEO of Cisco and a kingpin of the Internet]. Chambers said, The next killer application for the Internet is going to be education. Education over the Internet is going to be so big it is going to make email usage look like a rounding error." The quote was a relevant, validating, and compelling start for any company in that space (even though it turned out to be wrong).

The Aphorism

An *aphorism*, or familiar saying, can make for an excellent Opening Gambit. But be sure to select one that relates naturally and credibly to your main theme and your Point B.

Here are a few examples of Opening Gambit Aphorisms: I once worked on a biotechnology IPO with a company that was being formed by the merger of three smaller companies with related sciences in cancer research. The company launched its presentation with the following: "The whole is greater than the sum of its parts." The original axiom from Euclid, the founder of geometry, is "The whole is equal to the sum of its parts," but the biotech presenters gave the familiar saying a little twist. In doing so, they instantly identified the synergies that the new company would enjoy by combining competencies and resources.

Here are a few other examples:

A company that made graphic display screens used "Seeing is believing" to immediately express the clarity and fidelity of its unique products.

A company with a speech recognition technology used "Easier said than done."

A company that played in a niche market between two giant competitors used "Hit 'em where they ain't." This aphorism, attributed to old-time baseball great Wee Willie Keeler, is a pithy way of saying, "You don't have to be the biggest or the strongest to win in a competition; you can succeed simply by focusing on an area that others are ignoring."

In each case, the Opening Gambit Aphorism triggered the attention of the audience at the outset, allowing the presenter to move them into the heart of the presentation. Grab and navigate.

The Analogy

The final option, the Opening Gambit Analogy, is my personal favorite. An *analogy* is a comparison between two seemingly unrelated items. In the introduction to this book, I drew an analogy between a massage therapist and an effective presenter. I hope that got your attention.

A well-devised analogy is an excellent way of explaining anything that is arcane, obscure, or complicated. If your business deals with products, services, or systems that are technologically complex or require specialized knowledge to understand, look for a simple analogy that can allow audiences to grasp the essence of the story.

The simpler and clearer the analogy, the better. If you were trying to sell investors on a company that had developed improved software for data network management, you might explain your business by using a twist on a familiar comparison: "Think of us as the people who repair the potholes on the information superhighway. We plan to collect a toll from every driver who travels on our turnpike!"

Although the roadway analogy is a common choice for networking stories, I found an unusual variation of it for the IPO roadshow of a biotechnology company. TheraTech (now Watson Laboratories,

> 66 If your business deals with products, services, or systems that are technologically complex or require specialized knowledge to understand, look for a simple analogy that can allow audiences to grasp the essence of the story. 99

Inc., of Utah) had a technology that enabled controlled-release drug delivery through transdermal patches. During the roadshow preparations with Charles Ebert, TheraTech's vice president of research and development and a Ph.D. in pharmaceutics, he began to discuss the essentials of his core science. As Charles knowledgeably and thoroughly described TheraTech's matrix systems and permeation enhancers, I asked him to pause and explain those terms. Charles said, "Think of the matrix as a truck; think of the drug as its cargo; think of the skin as a border crossing where the truck has to stop; and think of the permeation enhancer as the motor that lifts the barrier and allows the truck to pass through."

Science is complex; by comparison, business is relatively simple. Often, it's difficult to combine the two. Even though the science behind the sequencing of the human genome is extremely complex, its business potential can be explained through an analogy: "Because our company's researchers were the first to locate and map the genes that cause several major diseases, we'll be in a position to require royalty payments from the big pharmaceutical firms working to eliminate those diseases. It's like owning the copyright on a hit song and collecting a royalty every time it is played."

Vince Mendillo is the director of worldwide marketing for Microsoft's Mobile Devices. He made the opening presentation at the Mobility Developers Conference in London that Microsoft organized for independent software vendors (ISVs) in Europe. ISVs write the applications that drive thousands of mobile devices as well as countless other software products.

Vince began his presentation with an Opening Gambit Analogy, made even more effective by leading up to it with this gracious greeting:

> Good morning! And since I am in Europe, I should add: Bonjour, Buenos dias, and as an Italian-American, Buon giorno!
>
> I'm also a history buff, and I've studied the history of the homeland of my ancestors. For centuries, Italy was divided into many autocratic and warring states. But in 1870, as a result of the valiant efforts of Giuseppe Garibaldi, a guerrilla fighter who became a great general, Italy became a unified nation.
>
> The mobile world today is very much like the Italy of yesterday, divided among autocratic warring factions. Now the battle is over technology, platforms, and systems. You ISVs are suffering from the results of that factionalism. We at Microsoft hear you and understand your confusion. In response, we've developed an ecosystem of partners that includes Intel, Texas Instruments, and major carriers, all involved with Microsoft to create an open platform that will enable its members to participate in the deployment of 100 million Microsoft mobile devices. We welcome you here today and invite you to become part of this ecosystem.

Vince's Opening Gambit was gracious, analogous, and unmistakably attention-getting.

Compound Opening Gambits

You can actually combine some of the previously mentioned options for your Opening Gambit. Remember from Part 1, "Your Point Is More Important Than PowerPoint," how Dan Warmenhoven, the CEO of Network Appliance, began his IPO roadshow: He started with the line "What's in a name?" (an aphorism: Juliet's immortal query to her Romeo). Then he asked, "What's an appliance?" (a rhetorical question, followed by the answer): "A toaster is an appliance." Then Dan used the toaster as an analogy: "A toaster does one thing and one thing well: It toasts bread."

With this triple Opening Gambit, Dan surely had his audience's attention, so he moved on to link the analogy to the rest of his presentation: "Managing data on networks is complicated. It is currently managed by devices that do many things, not all of them well. Our company, Network Appliance, makes a product called a file server. A file server does one thing and does it well: It manages data on networks." Now Dan was ready to move to his Point B: "When you think of the explosive growth of data in networks, you can see that our file servers are positioned to be a vital part of that growth, and Network Appliance is positioned to grow as a company. We invite you to join us in that growth."

Linking to Point B

To make the opening of your presentation as effective as possible, you need to do more than capture the interest of your audience. The optimal Opening Gambit goes further by linking to your Point B.

In every one of the previous examples, the presenters continued beyond the Opening Gambit and then hopped, skipped, and jumped along a path that concluded with Point B. To help you do the same, you need two additional stepping stones: the Unique Selling Proposition (USP) and the Proof of Concept.

USP

This is a very succinct summary of your business, the basic premise that describes what you or your company does, makes, or offers. Think of the USP as the "elevator" version of your presentation: the way you'd pitch yourself if you stepped into an elevator and suddenly saw that hot prospect you'd been trying to buttonhole. But please, make it a 4-story elevator ride, not a 70-story trip!

> 66 To make the opening of your presentation as effective as possible, you need to do more than capture the interest of your audience. The optimal Opening Gambit goes further by linking to your Point B. 99

The Unique Selling Proposition should be one or, at most, two sentences long. One of the most common complaints I hear about presentations is: "I listened to them for 30 minutes, and I still don't know what they do!" The USP is what they do.

> 66 The Unique Selling Proposition should be one or, at most, two sentences long. 99

Remember Dan Warmenhoven's opening: "Our company, Network Appliance, makes a product called a file server. A file server does one thing and does it well: It manages data on networks." A very clear, concise USP.

Proof of Concept

This is a single telling point that validates your USP. It gives instant credibility to your business. The Proof of Concept is optional. Sometimes you can start with the Opening Gambit, link through the USP, and then go directly to Point B without the extra beat.

It is a valuable beat, nonetheless, and when you do choose to include the Proof of Concept, you have a number of options. For example, you can use a significant sales achievement: "We sold 85,000 copies of this software the first day it was available"; a prestigious award: "*Business Week* picked our product as one of the top 10 of the year"; or an impressive endorsement: "When an IBM vice president tried our product, he told me he'd give anything if only IBM could have invented it."

Think of your Opening Gambit, USP, Proof of Concept, and Point B as dynamic inflection points. After you've segued smoothly through each of them at the start of your presentation, the heart of your argument is primed for your discussion. You will have grabbed your audience's attention, and they will be very clear about what you want them to do.

Set 'Em Up, and Knock 'Em Down

Let's go back to Scott Cook, the founding CEO of Intuit Software, and the presentation he made at the Robertson, Stephens and Company Technology Investment Conference prior to his public offering. Scott began with his two questions: "How many of you balance your checkbooks?" and "How many of you like doing it?"

As the chuckling subsided and all the hands dropped, Scott continued, "You're not alone. Millions of people around the world hate balancing their checkbooks. We at Intuit have developed a simple, easy-to-use, inexpensive, new personal finance tool called Quicken" (Intuit's USP). Now Scott started to roll: "We're confident that those millions of people who hate balancing their checkbooks will buy many units of Quicken...." Scott had built up such a head of steam that he skipped past his Proof of Concept and, without passing Go, went directly to his Point B: "...making Intuit a company you want to watch."

At that moment in the history of the company, Scott's sole purpose was to raise awareness among potential investors and investment managers for the upcoming Intuit IPO. Unlike the CEOs of other private companies presenting at the conference, all of whom were seeking financing, Scott was there only to tee up his roadshow: "...a company you want to watch." Scott was not there to raise capital. (In fact, at that very conference, Scott declined a handsome investment offer because he had all the working capital he needed from his primary investors, the Kleiner, Perkins, Caufield & Byers venture firm.)

As a footnote, Scott is never shy about asking for the order. Of the more than 400 CEOs I've coached for IPO roadshows, I've had to prompt almost all of them to make their call to action. (Remember that one of the Five Cardinal Sins is "What's your point?") Most CEOs are reluctant to use the *i* word (*invest*). Far be it for me to suggest that they do. Instead, I recommend words like *invite, join, participate,* and *share*. Only Scott Cook, among those 400, concluded his IPO roadshow by boldly asking, "Why should you invest in Intuit?" and then providing them with the answers.

Remember from Chapter 5, "Plotting Your Story: Flow Structures," how CEO Jerry Rogers began the Cyrix IPO roadshow: "Cyrix competes against the established giants Intel and AMD as well as two other large, well-funded companies." (Jerry's Opening Gambit was a factoid; in this case, a most striking statement.) "So as a tiny startup trying to establish itself, I have to respond to some challenging questions from potential new customers about the IBM-compatible microprocessors that Cyrix designs" (Cyrix's USP). "Three questions keep recurring: 'Will Cyrix microprocessors run all software applications?' 'How will Cyrix compete with Intel?' and 'Does Cyrix have the financial stability to succeed?'"

Jerry continued, "Cyrix has already begun shipments of the first commercially avail-able 486 microprocessors not produced by Intel" (Cyrix's Proof of Concept). "But those same three questions about compatibility, competition, and finances remain important to potential investors like you. In my presentation today, I'll provide you with the answers to those questions to demonstrate that Cyrix is indeed a sound investment" (Cyrix's Point B).

Jerry's answers and his call to action proved to be effective. When Cyrix launched as a public company, it was priced at $13 and the first trade was over $19—a signifi-cant achievement in 1993.

Now let's move from CEO Jerry Rogers to Carol Case, the salesperson from Argus Insurance you met earlier in this chapter. Carol began her pitches to her prospective buyers with the scenario about the fire. After the scenario, Carol continued, "Our customer is like many customers who purchase a basic policy not customized to their individual needs. She now realizes that means being just one stop away from disaster. Luckily, we at Argus Insurance have a solution. Argus can provide you with a customized, value-added package of insurance that provides for your individual needs to protect you against serious financial loss" (Argus's USP). Carol was already teeing up her Point B, but for good measure, she added her Proof of Concept: "Maybe that's why Argus is one of the fastest-growing insurance brokers in the state." Now, she was ready for an even stronger Point B: "I know that you'll want to take advantage of the opportunity and sign up for this important coverage today."

By power-launching your presentation with your Opening Gambit, USP, Proof of Concept, and Point B, your audience will have no doubt about where they're going. Now it's time for you to tell them how you intend to navigate them there.

Tell Them What You're Going to Tell Them

The dynamic inflection points mentioned previously will prime your audience, but do you want to now dive directly into the body of your presentation? Do you want to start drilling deeply into the first of the clusters you selected? Not quite yet. I suggest that first you take a moment to give your audience a preview of the outline of your major ideas.

The technique for helping your audience become oriented and track the flow of your ideas is the classic "tell 'em what you're gonna tell 'em." You can also think of it as the forest view.

In most business presentations, this preview is expressed in the overview or agenda slide. In an IPO roadshow, it's in the investment highlights slide. In either case, it summarizes the chief attractions of a company's offering. Why not map it to the sequence of the clusters? Why not make it track the entire presentation? In that way, you and your audience can see all the major clusters and the Flow Structure that unifies them. This is a view of both the trees and the forest. Think of it as a final quality check.

But telling your audience what you're gonna tell 'em has much more to offer than an agenda. You can also extend your narrative string with two more dynamic inflection points: linking forward from Point B and forecasting the running time of your presentation.

> 66 ...telling your audience what you're gonna tell 'em has much more to offer than an agenda. 99

Link Forward from Point B

In the Argus Insurance sales pitch, after Carol Case asked for the order with, "I know that you'll want to take advantage of the opportunity and sign up for this important coverage today," she continued on to her overview slide with, "...so that you can consider signing with Argus...," and then she ran through the bullets of her overview slide.

Contrast Carol's forward link with the far more common approach of no link at all: "Now I'd like to talk about my agenda...."

In the opening of the Intuit IPO roadshow presentation, after Scott Cook's call to action with, "Why should you invest in Intuit?", he made a forward link to his investment opportunity slide (shown in Figure 6.1) with, "These are the reasons to consider Intuit for your portfolio." Then he ran through the bullets, briefly adding value to each point.

FIGURE 6.1

What he's gonna tell 'em: Intuit's investment opportunity slide.

Investment Opportunity

- **Substantial, underpenetrated markets**
    - Personal finance
    - Small business accounting
    - International
    - Services
- **Proven consumer products approach**
- **Best of breed products**
- **Market share leader across all platforms**
- **Significant revenue from existing customers**

Intuit

In doing so, Scott avoided the all-too-common practice of reading the bullets verbatim; a practice that invariably annoys any audience because they think to themselves, "I'm not a child! I can read it myself!"

When Scott was done with the bullets, he added, "Please consider this the outline for the next 20 minutes of our presentation. Let's start at the top with the market opportunity," adding yet another forward link, this time into the heart of his presentation.

Forecast the Time

When you establish the endpoint at the beginning of your presentation, instead of plunging your audience headlong into a dark tunnel, they get to see the light at the end while they are still at the entrance. By stating the amount of time your presentation will take, you demonstrate that you are aware of the value of your audience's time and intend to use it productively—another aspect of audience advocacy.

By providing your audience with a *roadmap* and a *forecast* of the time, you are giving them a *plan* and a *schedule*. Those four italicized nouns have a least-common-denominator noun: management. Once again, you're sending the subliminal message of effective management.

> 66 By stating the amount of time your presentation will take, you demonstrate that you are aware of the value of your audience's time and intend to use it productively. 99

Of course, just because you've told 'em what you're gonna tell 'em, no one is going to think of you as an excellent manager. That's a stretch. But the converse proves the point: If you plunge your audience headlong into that dark tunnel without providing a roadmap or an endpoint, they'll feel out of control. If instead you show them the light, they'll sit back, lock into your message, and subconsciously say to themselves, "These people know what they're doing. They have a plan. They're well-prepared. Let's listen to what they have to say."

Telling 'em what you're gonna tell 'em also provides additional benefits to you, the presenter. When you click your overview slide and run through it for your audience, you can mentally check the components of your presentation and remind yourself of the overall flow of ideas. This will help you more easily move confidently from point to point as you step through the body of your presentation. Remember how well that worked for Hugh Martin of ONI Systems and his "Top 10 Questions from Institutional Investors"?

Furthermore, it's quite likely that someday, someone is going to come up to you five minutes before your presentation is due to begin and say, "Gee, I'm sorry, but we're running awfully late. We planned to give you half an hour, but we can only spare eight minutes."

Panic time? No. Simply move to your overview slide and walk your audience through your key points in the allotted time. After all, the overview slide is a miniature view of the entire presentation, so you can use it to support an ultra-brief condensation of all your ideas.

That old chestnut, "tell 'em what you're gonna tell 'em," has a host of benefits: roadmap, linkage, forecast, prompt, and short form.

You can now proceed to fulfill your forecast by telling 'em what you promised; that is, move through each of your clusters in greater detail, putting flesh on the sturdy bones of your structure.

Of course, when you're done with all the clusters, you then tell 'em what you told 'em. In most presentations, this is in the summary slide; in an IPO roadshow, it's in the investment highlights slide. In both cases, it's a mirror of its predecessor from the beginning of the presentation. This mirroring, this linking of the preview and the summary, serves to bookend the presentation. This also creates a thematic resolution that neatly ties together the entire presentation. Express that resolution with a final restatement of your Point B. The last words your audience should hear is your call to action.

> 66 The last words your audience should hear is your call to action. 99

An important footnote about your summary: Make it brief! In a book, when only a few pages are left and the reader knows the end is in sight, it is the writer's obligation to quicken the pace of the narrative. So it is with a presentation. When you get to your summary slide, be succinct.

You have now effectively grabbed your audience at the beginning, navigated them through all the parts, and deposited them at Point B. Moreover, your whole story has now fulfilled Aristotle's classical requirements for any story: a strong beginning, a solid middle, and a decisive end.

In my programs, I provide a story form (shown in Figure 6.2) that captures all of the above. It's a useful tool for tracking a basic format that will work for any persuasive presentation.

FIGURE 6.2

Presentation in a nutshell: the story form.

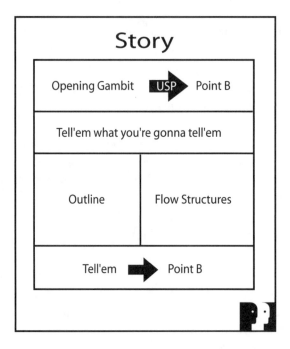

90 Seconds to Launch

The Opening Gambit, the USP, a forward link to Point B, another forward link to tell 'em, and one more forward link into the overview are the first important steps of any presentation. This continuous string creates a dynamic thrust that propels and energizes the balance of your time in front of your audience.

> 66 …if you capture your audience's attention, define your Point B, and establish your credibility in those same 90 seconds, the audience is yours and they will follow you wherever you want them to go. 99

It's important that you hit these points, in that order, within the first 90 seconds of your presentation, at the maximum. Always remember the importance of the start of your presentation. If you lose your audience within that first 90 seconds, chances are that they will be lost forever. You never get a second chance to make a first impression.

But if you capture your audience's attention, define your Point B, and establish your credibility in those same 90 seconds, the audience is yours and they will follow you wherever you want them to go.

CASE STUDY: A TOUGH CROWD

Jim Flautt was the vice president of marketing at DigitalThink, and he participated in the program I delivered to help Mike Pope, the newly ascended CEO, develop a presentation to announce the company's new strategic focus.

The day after the program, Jim attended a presentation at the alumni association of his graduate business school. Jim decided to watch from the back of the room, as I told him I always do, to observe not only the presenter, but the audience reaction as well. The guest speaker was a respected industry leader and a frequent presenter, but his presentation was, from the outset, an unabated torrent of excessive words and slides. Jim could see that the audience quickly lost interest: MEGO. As he watched the shifting heads and squirming bodies in front of him, Jim smiled knowingly to himself. He understood exactly what had gone wrong.

The very next day, Jim, who happens to be an Annapolis graduate and a former naval officer aboard the USS Albany, was scheduled to speak about submarines to his son's first-grade class at Laurel Elementary School. Jim realized that a roomful of seven-year-olds, who represent the ultimate in short attention spans, would be as challenging as any business audience. So, he set about to make use of what he'd learned about making business presentations to prepare for the first graders.

continues

In the style of Intuit's Scott Cook, Jim began with a call-for-a-show-of-hands Opening Gambit, a format quite familiar to his young audience. Jim had three questions: "How many of you know what a submarine is?" All the first graders raised their hands. "How many of you have ever seen a submarine?" Half the first graders raised their hands. "How many of you have ever seen a submarine fly?" Now all the first graders smiled, giggled, and gasped. Jim had their attention.

Jim continued on to his Point B: "Well, I'm here today to tell you all about submarines." Then, to link forward from his Point B, Jim told 'em what he was gonna tell 'em: "...what goes on in a submarine, how to drive a submarine, how to repair a submarine, and some cool things that a submarine does. When I'm done with all of that, about 15 minutes from now..." (Jim's forecast for time) "...I'm going to show you a submarine that flies!" Just for good measure, Jim added a big WIIFY.

This got more smiles, giggles, gasps, and now delighted cheers from the children. Jim had them and he kept them, with simple slide photographs, in rapt attention for about 15 minutes, until the very end. Then, true to his promise, Jim clicked on his computer and ran a video clip of a U.S. Navy submarine going through an emergency surfacing exercise, leaping up out of the roiling ocean looking, for all the world, like a dolphin performing a stunt.

Jim did it all: He grabbed, navigated, and deposited. If it can work with wired seven-year-olds, it can work with occupationally short-attention-span investors looking to make a return on their investments, with a concerned customer looking to find a product that performs a vital function better than the current solution, or with a stressed manager looking for a strategy to compete more effectively. It can work for you.

The Absolute Minimum

- By power-launching your presentation with your Opening Gambit, your USP, your Proof of Concept, and your Point B, your audience will have no doubt about where they're going.

- That old chestnut "tell 'em what you're gonna tell 'em" has a host of benefits: roadmap, linkage, forecast, prompt, and short form.

- The last words your audience should hear is your call to action.

PART III

SHOWING YOUR STORY

- The problem with presentations-as-documents

- Getting the audience to look at you, not your slides

- Making more out of less with simple design and minimal eye sweeps

7

COMMUNICATING VISUALLY

Think about a time when you were in the audience at a presentation and the graphics didn't work. What was the problem? The most common answers I get when I ask my business clients this question include

- The graphics were cluttered.
- There was too much on the slide.
- The slide looked like an eye chart.
- The slide was a Data Dump.

Visually, It's a Dump

Now flip the lens and take the point of view of an audience advocate. What's the effect on you? It's another case of the dreaded MEGO syndrome: the same cause and effect as when a story is unloaded on you as a Data Dump.

The main reason this happens is that presenters fail to distinguish between a document and a presentation. They treat a presentation as a document. Business *documents* include annual reports, filled with dense text and highly detailed tables, charts, and graphs; strategic plans, filled with dense text and highly detailed tables, charts, and graphs; market analyses, filled with dense text and highly detailed tables, charts, and graphs; and meeting notes, filled with dense text and highly detailed tables, charts, and graphs. All these types of documents are necessary and important in their place, but business documents are not presentations.

The Proper Role of Graphics

So, the true problem with presentation graphics is that, all too often, presenters take a flood of data (yes, those dense texts with highly detailed tables, charts, and graphs) and simply reproduce them, with little or no modification, for their presentation graphics.

I call this the Presentation-As-Document Syndrome, and it represents one of the most common underlying problems that plague presentations. Presenters have become so accustomed to relying on graphics, especially Microsoft PowerPoint slides, that they often think of the presentation as a mere accompaniment to those aids. In fact, many people act as if the presentation is completely dispensable. "Jerry," they'll say, "I can't attend your presentation next week. But it doesn't matter. Just send me your slides." Or they sometimes say, "Send me your slides in advance." The PowerPoint slides then are treated as handouts. Just because PowerPoint offers to "convert" business documents into slides doesn't mean it's a good idea.

What's more, presenters frequently provide the handouts to their audience before the presentation. The audience then reads the handout, sees the slide, and hears the presenter read what is on the slide. This is known as *triple delivery*, an assault on the audience's senses that leads to that lethal MEGO.

> 66 Presenters have become so accustomed to relying on graphics, especially Microsoft PowerPoint slides, that they often think of the presentation as a mere accompaniment to those aids. 99

Using slides as handouts is but one manifestation of the Presentation-As-Document Syndrome. There are three other examples:

- Using the slides as notes to help the presenter remember what to say

- Cramming a plethora of details on the slides as if to demonstrate legitimacy

- Filling the slides with enough information so that anyone else in the company using the same slides will maintain the uniformity of the message

> 66 A presentation is a presentation and only a presentation, and *never* a document. 99

Please note that the name of my business is not Power Handouts, Power Notes, Power Details, or Power Uniformity. It is Power Presentations.

A presentation is a pure play. It must serve only one purpose. Remember the words of Dan Warmenhoven, the CEO of Network Appliance, in the Opening Gambit of his IPO roadshow, "Do one thing and one thing well." If a presentation tries to serve two or more purposes, it dilutes both purposes. The presentation itself is neither fish nor fowl.

A presentation is a presentation and only a presentation, and *never* a document. After all, Microsoft provides Word for documents and PowerPoint for presentations. And never the twain shall meet.

If you do need a document of your presentation, PowerPoint provides the Notes Page view (see Figure 7.1). The top of the Notes Page contains only what your audience sees projected on the screen; the bottom provides the additional material for the handouts.

FIGURE 7.1

The takeaway....

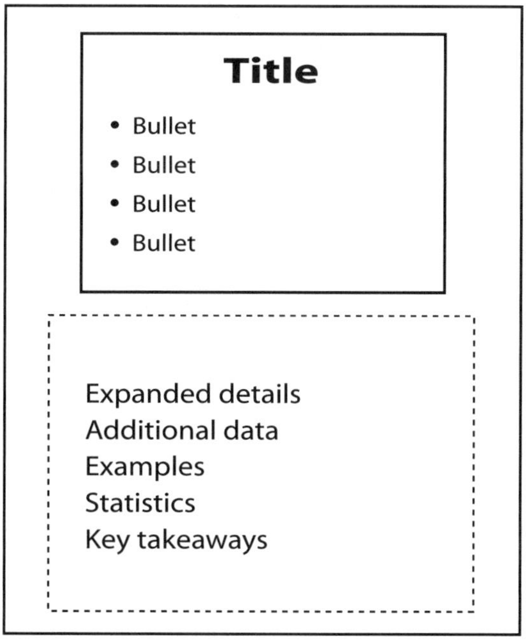

Title
- Bullet
- Bullet
- Bullet
- Bullet

Expanded details
Additional data
Examples
Statistics
Key takeaways

Be sure to distribute the handouts only *after* the presentation. If you distribute them before or during the presentation, your audience members will be flipping through them as you speak, and they won't listen to what you have to say.

> 66 Be sure to distribute the handouts only *after* the presentation. 99

If you're asked to provide a copy of your presentation for a conference so the slides can be printed in book form, use the PowerPoint Notes Page view. That way, you'll maintain the integrity of your slides as purely presentation material.

If you're asked to provide a copy of the presentation in advance, as so often happens, especially in the venture capital and financial business, politely offer to provide a business plan or executive summary as a document. And, create that document with Microsoft Word and not PowerPoint.

Presenter Focus

An extension of the Presentation-As-Document Syndrome is what happens to the audience when the screen lights up with a slide filled with dense text and highly detailed tables, charts, and graphs. The focus of the audience immediately—and involuntarily—goes to the graphics and they start to read. When they start reading, they stop listening. The graphics then become the center of attention and the presenter becomes subordinate to the slideshow, serving, at best, as a voice-over narrator and, at worst, as a ventriloquist.

This problem is compounded as the presenter becomes a reader, too. The reading often fails to rise above the level of a verbatim recitation. Reciting the slides verbatim is patronizing to the audience. They think to themselves, "I'm not a child! I can read it myself!" The results are a failure to connect, a failure to communicate, and most likely a failure to persuade.

An even worse variant is when the presenter rambles, talking about subjects that are not on the slide. In effect, this jams the audience's audio and video channels, resulting in confusion and annoyance.

My approach is different.

I view graphics the way my clients at Microsoft view them. The Executive Presentations Team is the specialized unit at Microsoft charged with producing the slides and graphics necessary to support the senior executives at major presentation events for the company. It's headed by Jon Bromberg, who is

> 66 Reciting the slides verbatim is patronizing to the audience. 99

my friend and an alumnus of the New York theatrical world. Today, Jon is the director of events in charge of a huge operation with state-of-the-art production capabilities worthy of CBS, Disney, or the Broadway theater for television, audio, Internet, and live presentations.

> 66 The slides or other graphics are there to support the presenter, not the other way around. 99

Significantly, the Executive Presentations Team refers to PowerPoint, Microsoft's own product, as speaker support. The slides or other graphics are there to support the presenter, not the other way around.

This is the very same model that we see every evening on the network news broadcasts. We see the anchor—Peter Jennings, Dan Rather, or Tom Brokaw—presenting information he interprets for us. Yes, he uses graphics, but his graphics play a supporting role. The images often consist of little more than a simple picture and a word or two to headline the story the anchor is presenting: a photograph of the Capitol building and the words "Tax Debate" or a picture of a medicine bottle and the words "Prescription Drugs." Jennings, Rather, or Brokaw is always center-stage.

It so happens that my cousin, Joel Goldberg, has worked for 25 years as a graphic artist at ABC News. Using elaborate electronic tools, Joel often spends an hour getting the appearance of a single image or word exactly right, with highlights, tints, dimension, shadowing, and other tricks of his trade. That image or word might appear on the screen behind Peter Jennings for just a few seconds before vanishing forever. While I'm sure that Joel is paid well for his talents, it is Peter Jennings who pulls down a seven-figure salary for the credibility he brings to the news.

This presenter focus/graphics support relationship is the only effective model for a presentation. The presentation cannot serve as a document unless it is complete in itself, in which case, the audience wouldn't need the presenter. They could sit in silence and read the slides to themselves. On the other hand, if the graphics constitute a partial document, they cannot stand alone and serve only to distract attention from the presenter. Yet another expression of the neither-fish-nor-fowl dilemma.

Instead, when the presenter interprets for the audience and the graphics provide support, the presenter can then lead the audience to a conclusion. When this happens, the presenter manages the audience's minds, creating the subliminal takeaway: effective management.

The audience also takes away a visual reinforcement of the presenter's message.

As an ancient Chinese proverb tells us:

> 66 The presentation cannot serve as a document unless it is complete in itself, in which case, the audience wouldn't need the presenter. 99

I hear and I forget;

I see and I remember;

I do and I understand.

Less Is More

To make all this happen, we need a guiding principle. That principle is "Less Is More." These words have been attributed to one of the foremost architects and designers of the twentieth century, Ludwig Mies van der Rohe (1886–1969), the father of the minimalist school. However, Less Is More existed before Mies was born, in Robert Browning's 1855 poem, "Andrea del Sarto."

> 66 Less Is More should be your guiding principle when you are creating your presentation graphics. 99

Mies directed the influential Bauhaus School of Design in Germany in the 1930s and then came to the United States, where he designed such sleek, classic structures as the bronze-and-glass Seagram Building in New York City.

Mies's famous Less Is More dictum became the guiding principle for many of the greatest designers of the past hundred years. Less Is More should be your guiding principle when you are creating your presentation graphics.

It is mine. It is mine after years of working in television, with access to the vast capabilities of professional graphic artists like my cousin Joel, operating in multimillion-dollar control rooms called "electronic paint pots." It is mine after almost 15 years of working with evolving generations of computer-based graphics programs, culminating in the XP version of Microsoft's PowerPoint, whose capabilities approach those of the professional electronic paint pots. It's good to have all those powerful tools available to me. But when designing graphics, I've learned to rely on the wisdom of Less Is More and its corollary, "When in Doubt, Leave It Out."

An important benefit of a slide designed with this minimalist approach is that it serves as an instant prompt for the presenter: a visual mnemonic.

Perception Psychology

In addition to presenter focus and Less Is More, the two essential concepts for powerful graphics design, there is a third vital element in the equation: the audience and how they take in what they see. I call this perception psychology.

Let's begin by analyzing how the human eye moves.

You're familiar with the illuminated initial letter that appears in fine manuscripts or in handsomely printed books. It always appears in the upper-left corner of the page, where a new book or a new chapter begins. Magazines and newspapers also often use an enlarged initial letter to start articles. That's because in western countries such as the United States, France, Spain, and Germany, languages are always printed from left to right and top to bottom. As a result, a western reader's eyes are conditioned to move to the upper-left corner to start a new passage.

This is not innate. It's culturally determined and learned. In the Middle East, books begin at the back and are read from right to left. Therefore, the eyes of those readers are conditioned to begin at the upper-right corner of a page.

> 66 ...a western reader's eyes are conditioned to move to the upper-left corner to start a new passage. 99

I call this tendency for our eyes to jump to the upper-left corner of a page the *conditioned carriage return* because the movement recalls the repeated movement of the carriage on an old-fashioned typewriter.

When people read print in a book, magazine, or newspaper, their eyes make the conditioned carriage return with every new page. In a presentation, this movement occurs with every new slide.

There is one major difference, however. When your eyes shuttle across a page in a book or magazine, they move only 5"–8" at a time. In a presentation, when they have to leap across a large screen in a conference room or auditorium, they move anywhere from 2 feet to 20 feet, depending on the size of the screen.

Therefore, every time a new graphic flashes on the screen, here's what happens: First, because of a lifetime of conditioning, the eyes of the audience jump to the upper-left corner. Then their eyes suddenly become aware that there is more information on the screen, so now their eyes must make another move to take in the rest of the information. This next move is more powerful than the first. Their eyes sweep to the right in a completely involuntary action. I call this the *reflexive cross sweep*, illustrated in Figure 7.2.

FIGURE 7.2

The reflexive cross sweep.

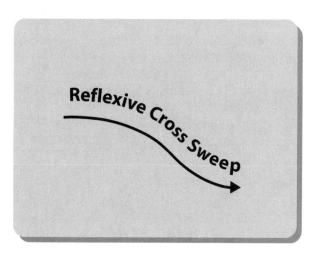

Unlike the learned move of the conditioned carriage return, the left-to-right movement of the reflexive cross sweep is apparently innate. Sometimes the move is down and to the right, and sometimes it is up and to the right. Most painters organize their pictures based on eye movement down and to the right. That is why, more often than not, artists sign their canvases in the lower-right corner.

Businesspeople also intuitively follow the reflexive move to the right; but they are also accustomed to taking the high road, following the desired growth pattern of revenue and profits symbolized by the hockey stick (see Figure 7.3).

FIGURE 7.3

The hockey-stick movement.

Whether up and to the right (as in business) or down and to the right (as in art), this involuntary left-to-right movement is deeply embedded in our nature.

No one has ever fully explained why these reflexive movements occur. In his 1954 book *Art and Visual Perception: A Psychology of the Creative Eye*, Rudolf Arnheim, a Gestalt psychologist and a scholar of art and cinema, offered several theories, ranging from the plausible to the fanciful. The plausible: Because the majority of humans are right-handed, there is a natural tendency toward greater awareness of objects on the right side of the visual field. The fanciful: Early humans were so impressed by the movement of the sun from left to right that they favored this form of movement. (Why fanciful? Well, it applies only to humans living north of the equator, and because most modern anthropologists now believe our earliest ancestors originated in Africa, south of the equator, that theory is dubious.)

> 66 Whether up and to the right (as in business) or down and to the right (as in art), this involuntary left-to-right movement is deeply embedded in our nature. 99

All these theories notwithstanding, the innate predisposition of the eye to move from left to right is undeniable. It is palpable. You can feel it yourself as you scan this very page or any of the illustrations in this book.

> 66 A pan right is smooth; a pan left drags. 99

In my days in television, I incorporated this preference in how I directed subjects and cameras. Next time you watch a well-directed movie or television drama, notice how the characters move across the screen. Most often, the sympathetic characters, the heroes and heroines with whom the audience identifies, move from the left side of the screen toward the right, flowing with the natural movement of the eye. By contrast, the unsympathetic characters, the villains whom the audience dislikes, move from right to left, fighting against the eye's natural flow.

Even when the characters are stationary, the movement of the camera can convey the same feelings: A pan right is smooth; a pan left drags. Very subtly, these differences fuel the audience's emotional reaction to the drama, helping them to think and feel the way the actors, director, and writer intended.

Director Sam Mendes used these techniques to powerful effect in the Tom Hanks/Paul Newman film *The Road to Perdition*. In the opening scene, we see a city street in the Depression era crowded with pedestrians, most of them moving from left to right. Then a young boy on a bicycle enters, pedaling from right to left, struggling against the grain. The boy is Tom Hanks's son, whose difficulties form the central part of the story. From the outset, these powerful cinematic dynamics set the foreboding tone for the entire film.

In the theater, directors incorporate the same approach with actors on the stage: Protagonists move toward the right, and antagonists move toward the left.

It all goes back to how we first learned to absorb information as children: reading text. By understanding perception psychology and applying it properly, you can control the effect of your graphics on your audience. And in presentations, you want that effect to be positive.

In a presentation, when a new image flashes on the screen, within an instant, the eyes of your audience will make two moves: one to the left to start the slide (the conditioned carriage return) and one to the right to take in all the information (the reflexive cross sweep). The move to the right will go either up or down.

> 66 By understanding perception psychology and applying it properly, you can control the effect of your graphics on your audience. 99

However, if in the design of your graphics, you've put excess data on the screen, your audience cannot finish in two moves. They're forced to make another trip, and perhaps more than one. This third move, along with any subsequent trips they must make, will be hard work, backwards and against the grain. I call this third trip, back and to the left, the *forced carriage return*. You can see all three moves in Figure 7.4.

FIGURE 7.4

An eye-roller: Three moves caused by excessive graphic information.

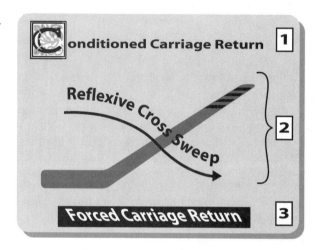

This again leads us to one of the most important practical applications of the Less Is More dictum: Don't Make Me Think! That refrain asks you not to make your audience work to understand your ideas. The same refrain applies to the work your audience must do to absorb your graphics. Therefore, design all your slides to minimize the eye sweeps of your audience. For every graphic, keep the number of times their eyes must go back and forth across the screen to an absolute minimum. Make it easy for your audience and they will be receptive to you.

Thus, the overarching principles of powerful and effective graphics are

- Presenter focus
- Less Is More
- Minimize eye sweeps

Everything that follows explains how to implement these principles.

Graphic Design Elements

All the bells and whistles in all the graphics programs available for business presentations boil down to just four basic design elements:

- **Pictorial**—Photographs, sketches, maps, icons, logos, screen shots, or clip art.

- **Relational**—Tables, matrices, hierarchies, and organizational charts. (Think of a relational chart as an image that captures a set of relationships, connections, or links in visual form.)

> 66 When you choose either pictorial or relational, you achieve Less Is More by default. 99

- **Text**—Text comes in two flavors: bullets and sentences.

- **Numeric**—Numbers expressed in bar charts, pie charts, area charts, line charts, histograms, and other more specialized types of graphs.

When you choose either pictorial or relational, you achieve Less Is More by default. A picture is worth a thousand words. And a table or chart, by definition, organizes multiple diverse elements, turning more into less. So, both pictorial and relational graphics instantly fulfill Mies van der Rohe's principle.

However, a lot of business information can't be captured in a picture or table. As a result, most presentations bulk up with text and numeric graphics. This is where the trouble begins. In the first place, presenters wind up using more, not less, on the screen, thereby losing effectiveness. What's worse, they fall prey to the Presentation-As-Document Syndrome.

A presentation is a presentation and only a presentation. The primary role of graphics is to support the presenter and give the presenter the opportunity to add value above and beyond what is projected on the screen.

Graphics also help the audience remember your content. Remember the Chinese proverb "I see and I remember."

In the next chapter, you learn how to create effective text graphics, and in the one after that, you learn how to create effective numeric graphics. The emphasis in both of these chapters is on how to achieve Less Is More, thereby conveying your visual information in a clear, crisp, and powerful form.

THE ABSOLUTE MINIMUM

- A presentation is a presentation and only a presentation, and never a document.

- Less Is More should be your guiding principle when you are creating your presentation graphics.

- Design all your slides to minimize the eye sweeps of your audience.

8

MAKING THE TEXT TALK

In the previous chapter, you saw that all text slides come in only two varieties: bullets and sentences. Each of these options is quite different, with separate forms and functions. Keep them distinct.

Bullets Versus Sentences

A bullet is used to express a core idea. It takes the form of a headline. Look at any newspaper and you'll see that a headline is not a complete sentence. Basic English grammar tells us that a sentence must contain a subject and a verb, but many headlines don't contain a subject and a verb. Generally, headlines don't use all the parts of speech that complete sentences contain: articles (*the, an, a*), conjunctions (*and, but, or*), and prepositions (*of, for, by, through*).

> **"** A bullet is used to express a core idea. **"**

Why are headlines written in this shorthand style? There are several good reasons. When fewer words have to be squeezed into an available space, the size of the letters can be increased, enhancing legibility. Furthermore, by providing the gist of the story in a few words, readers can scan a page full of stories in a few seconds and pick out the ones of interest.

The same benefits—legibility and speed—apply to bullets in presentation slides. When you create a text slide containing bullets, you are, in effect, presenting headlines only. Where does the body text appear? Not on any slide. As the presenter, it's your job to put flesh on the bones of the headline bullets. The presenter provides the body text. The presenter is the focus of the presentation.

This approach can make for a very crisp, clear presentation. You can summarize most of the concepts of your story (distilled in the brainstorming process and organized into clusters) in two- to five-word headline-style bullets. Some typical concepts from any company story might include

- Breakthrough New Product Line
- Experienced Management Team
- Exploding Market
- Targeted Strategy

How long would you be able to speak about any of these concepts as they apply to your business? Probably for several minutes each, if not longer. The optimal presentation, then, consists of the presenter providing the spoken body text for the headline-style bullets on the slides.

> **"** As the presenter, it's your job to put flesh on the bones of the headline bullets. **"**

Then what about sentences? When should you use them in your graphics?

The only time you need a sentence is when you need to demonstrate verbatim accuracy. Use a sentence only when you're citing the specific words in a quotation, like this:

> "PQR Technologies is the most exciting new business concept I've seen this year."
>
> —Tom Hudson, *High-Tech Monthly*

66 The only time you need a sentence is when you need to demonstrate verbatim accuracy. **99**

Although full sentences are acceptable for quotations, most well-crafted presentations keep them to a minimum, relying primarily on bullets as headlines for text slides.

An important underlying reason for avoiding sentences on slides goes back to the basic principle of audience advocacy. Sentences are longer than bullets, and they usually extend over several lines. Therefore, reading them on the slide generally requires additional eye sweeps, making your audience work harder to absorb your message. Make it easy for the audience to take in your graphics. Minimize eye sweeps.

Wordwrap

When a bullet is too long to fit on a single line, the text automatically continues on to a second line. This is called *wordwrap*, and it looks like Figure 8.1.

FIGURE 8.1

Too much work: Wordwrap forces two eye sweeps.

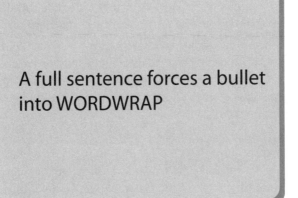

A full sentence forces a bullet into WORDWRAP

A full sentence almost always causes wordwrap, which requires an extra eye sweep—and more work for the audience. Shift the sentence-style bullet to a headline-style bullet by omitting articles, conjunctions, prepositions, and other unnecessary words. Minimize the eye sweeps by restricting the bullet to a single line.

66 Minimize the eye sweeps by restricting the bullet to a single line. **99**

Crafting the Effective Bullet Slide

You'll recall that I use the Problem/Solution Flow Structure in my programs and in this book. In most of the previous chapters, I've begun by asking you to think about presentation problems. In the same spirit, let's look at a particularly problematic bullet slide, shown in Figure 8.2.

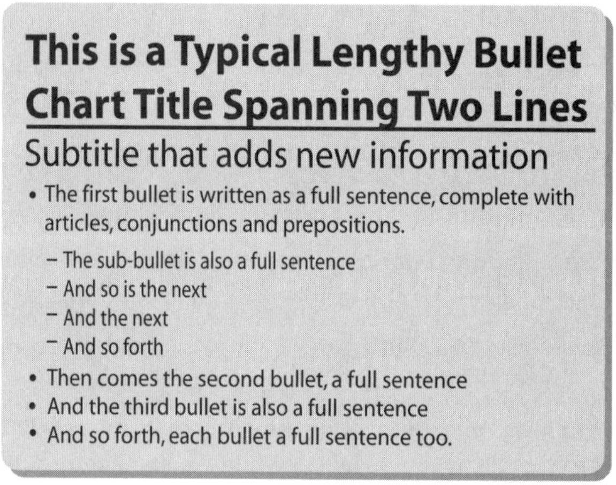

FIGURE 8.2

How not to design a bullet slide.

This is a Typical Lengthy Bullet Chart Title Spanning Two Lines
Subtitle that adds new information

- The first bullet is written as a full sentence, complete with articles, conjunctions and prepositions.
  - The sub-bullet is also a full sentence
  - And so is the next
  - And the next
  - And so forth
- Then comes the second bullet, a full sentence
- And the third bullet is also a full sentence
- And so forth, each bullet a full sentence too.

Does this look familiar? When I show this slide during my program, the groans and laughter from the participants make it clear that slides like this are all too common. This is a true data dump slide, one that is desperately in need of surgery.

First, consider the two-line title. It requires an extra eye sweep. In this book, your eyes traverse a page that is only a few inches wide. In your presentations, the eyes of your audience will have to travel several feet across a large projection screen. The more you make the eyes of your audience travel, the harder they have to work. Be an audience advocate! Replace the two-line title with a one-liner that states a single concept.

Next, notice that the subtitle, which adds new information, makes the audience do extra work not only to interpret the new information, but also to determine its relationship to the main title. Instead, replace it with a subtitle that relates easily and obviously back to the main title. Better still, eliminate the subtitle altogether. Less Is More.

Next, consider the first bullet. It's written with all the parts of speech that make a bullet into a sentence. This gives the audience more work to do by adding extra eye sweeps. Simplify the bullet into a

> 66 Replace the two-line title with a one-liner that states a single concept. 99

newspaper-style headline. Do the same with all the other bullets and with the sub-bullets as well.

Now for a subtle but important point: The default in most graphics and word processing programs is to mark a sub-bullet with a dash. This means that several sub-bullets create a ladder of dashes. What does a dash mean to a financial person? It is a minus sign, which means a negative.

> 66 Avoid the subtle, subconscious, negative message sent by the dash. 99

You don't want your audience to go there. Avoid the subtle, subconscious, negative message sent by the dash. You could change the default symbol to a dot, which is an improvement, but it still clutters the slide. Get rid of the Morse-code effect of dots or dashes completely by tabbing the sub-bullets. The space creates the offset; the space makes less out of more.

Finally, do we really need all those sub-bullets? The answer is usually "no." Sub-bullets often add a layer of complexity and an extra burden for the audience without any offsetting benefit. Remember, you the presenter provide the body text. You'll have ample opportunity during your presentation to spell out the details that support the headline bullets.

Now we have a clean graphic, as you can see in Figure 8.3.

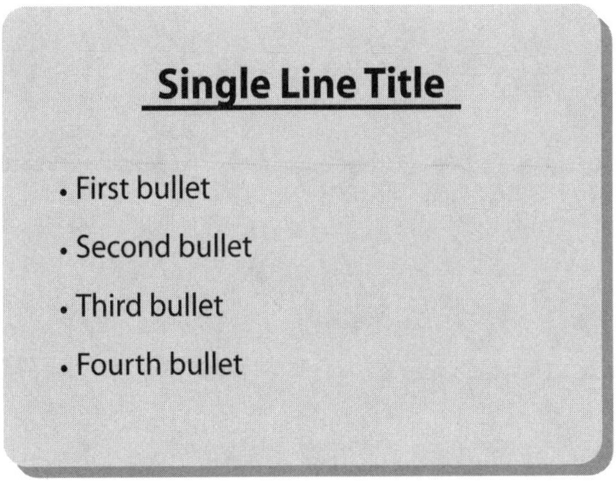

FIGURE 8.3

Aaah: The Less Is More bullet slide.

Single Line Title

- First bullet
- Second bullet
- Third bullet
- Fourth bullet

To summarize:

■ The Less Is More bullet slide contains one concept, expressed in a one-line title.

■ The subtitle has been omitted.

■ Bullets contain only key words, such as nouns, verbs, and modifiers. Avoid using articles, conjunctions, and prepositions.

> 66 Sub-bullets often add a layer of complexity and an extra burden for the audience without any offsetting benefit. 99

(Especially avoid using prepositions; not only do they add an extra word, but they also juxtapose and separate important words. Instead of writing a bullet such as "Strengths of our Company," rewrite it as "Our Company Strengths.")

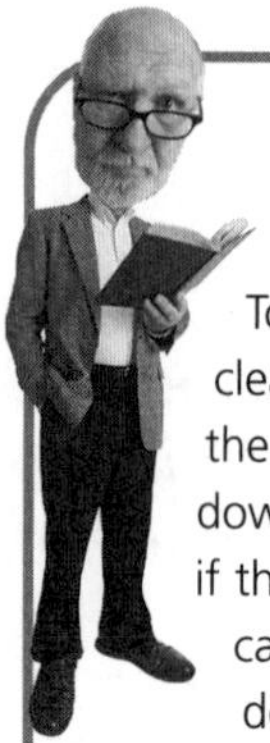

Minimize Eye Sweeps with Parallelism

When all your bullets are parallel or similar in meaning (for example, a list of products, product features, or product benefits), the relationships are immediately clear to your audience. However, whenever you create such a parallel list, pay particular attention to the grammatical form of the bullets. If you write each one in a different part of speech, you'll be forcing your audience to do extra work to grasp the logic. They'll have to reset their minds at the start of each bullet, as you do when you read the list in Figure 8.4.

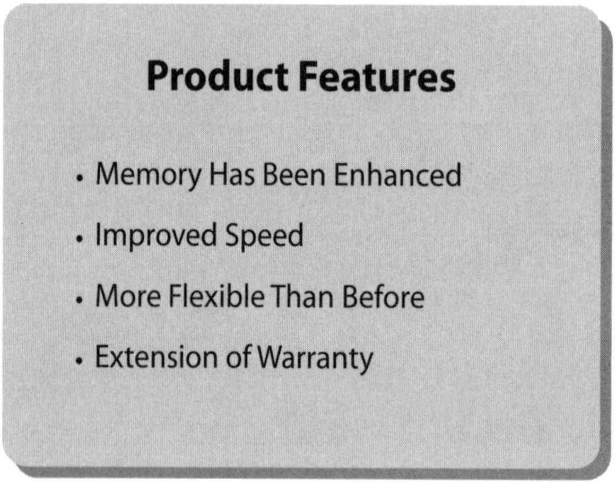

tip

To make your bullet slide clean and crisp, try to follow the 4 × 4 formula: four lines down, four words across. Or, if the subject warrants, you can go up to 6 × 4: six lines down, but still only four words across. A final benefit: With only one set of bullet symbols, visible at the first glance, both you and your audience get a quick snapshot of the total.

FIGURE 8.4

Diagram this: Bullets in non-parallel form.

Product Features

- Memory Has Been Enhanced
- Improved Speed
- More Flexible Than Before
- Extension of Warranty

Don't make me think! Each of these bullets represents a different grammatical form. The first bullet is a complete sentence with a passive verb; the second bullet is a noun modified by a preceding adjective; the third bullet is an adjective modified by a preceding adverb; and so on. Grammatical terminology notwithstanding, you can feel the inconsistency.

This problem is akin to the "floating decimal" dilemma in accounting, in which a series of figures is printed with irregular decimal places. This makes the numbers very difficult to read and compare accurately, anathema to any bookkeeper or accountant. In bullet slides, nonparallel construction of bullets is anathema to your audience's comprehension.

> 66 To solve this problem, write any set of bullets in a list in parallel form, so the similarity and relationships of the underlying concepts are obvious. 99

To solve this problem, write any set of bullets in a list in parallel form (grammatically structured the same way), so the similarity and relationships of the underlying concepts are obvious, as in Figure 8.5.

FIGURE 8.5

Adjective + noun: The same bullets in grammatically parallel form.

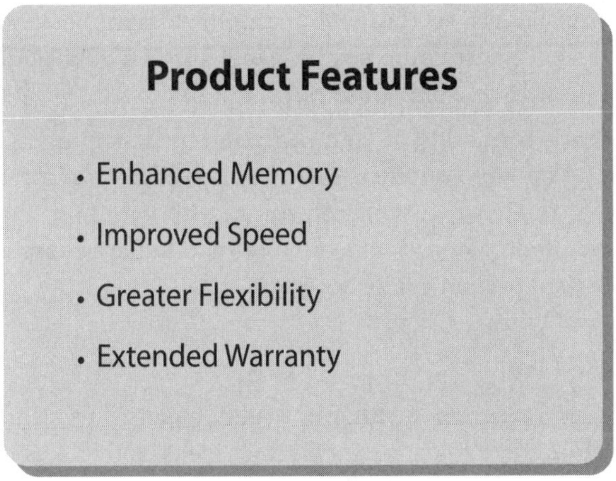

Product Features

- Enhanced Memory
- Improved Speed
- Greater Flexibility
- Extended Warranty

In Figure 8.5, each of the bullets is in the same grammatical form: adjective + noun. This parallelism in both meaning and form makes it easy for your audience to see the relationships. With this organization, you can display all four bullets at once. Your audience can absorb them quickly and then turn their attention back to you to listen as you add value.

Using the Build

Sometimes parallelism isn't applicable, so the relationships among the bullets are not readily apparent. And sometimes, a single concept requires more than four bullets; it might take five or six or even eight bullets to fully explain one main concept. But

> 66 This parallelism in both meaning and form makes it easy for your audience to see the relationships. 99

throwing a diverse or a multiplicity of bullets on the screen at once is too much input for your audience's eyes and minds. It overwhelms their reception.

The effective solution for either case is to build the list, one bullet at a time. The build is easy to do with the Custom Animation feature in Microsoft PowerPoint or any other presentation graphics program. Reveal the first line and explain and discuss it. Then click to reveal the next line and explain and discuss it, until you reveal all the bullets.

tip

In the XP version of Microsoft PowerPoint, you can accomplish this by selecting Custom Animation, Entrance, Wipe, From Left.

When building your bullets, keep in mind perception psychology: Audiences find left-to-right movement natural and easy. Make it easy for your audience. Build your bullets by bringing them in from left to right.

As you build, provide continuity in your narration by describing the relationships as you move from one bullet to another. You can also control the revelation of your bullets, keeping the audience in synchronization with your flow. They cannot get ahead of you. Best of all, you can add value to each bullet by discussing, interpreting, and providing supporting evidence.

Bullet Levels

Some presenters are not satisfied with one level of bullets, so they use sub-bullets, thinking this enables them to elaborate on their ideas. Sometimes this doesn't seem to be enough, so they use sub-sub-bullets. Occasionally, presenters completely surrender to temptation, and they go deeper, and deeper, and deeper, and deeper—all the way down into the right brain basement (see Figure 8.6). The trouble is that most audiences can't follow the presenter's mind that far down.

Do your audience a favor: Restrict yourself to one sub-bullet level only. A single level of sub-bullets (or no sub-bullets at all) keeps slides clear, crisp, and easy to read. It avoids forcing the audience into mental contortions as they struggle to track your own internal logic. Additionally, avoid the Morse-code effect by using no symbols for sub-bullets, only an indent to create a space. Less Is More.

> 66 Audiences find left-to-right movement natural and easy. Build your bullets by bringing them in from left to right. 99

FIGURE 8.6

How low can
you go? Multiple
levels of sub-
bullets.

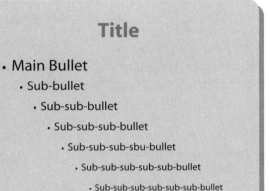

If you do use sub-bullets, distribute the same number to each bullet, as in Figure 8.7.
If the first bullet carries two sub-bullets, every other bullet should carry two sub-bullets. The resulting symmetry creates a balanced image, as well as the message
that your ideas are logical. The visual organization sends a subliminal message of
effective management.

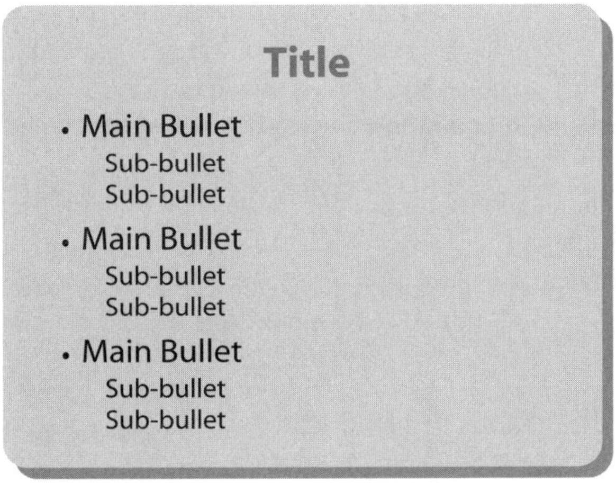

FIGURE 8.7

Bullet balance:
One level of sub-
bullets only.

Verbal Style

Now for some stylistic techniques that apply to all text slides, whether they contain bullets or sentences. These are seemingly minor points your audience might never consciously notice, but they have a definite subconscious impact on them and on how they perceive your slide and therefore your message. Follow these simple and straightforward style guidelines whenever you create text slides.

> 66 Restrict yourself to one sub-bullet level only....Additionally, avoid the Morse-code effect by using no symbols for sub-bullets, only an indent to create a space. 99

Use Possessives/Plurals Correctly and Sparingly, If at All

This is a grammatical and stylistic point that surprisingly few people understand. The use of an apostrophe plus *s* (*'s*) to mark the plural form is simply wrong. Incorrect. Bad English. No exceptions. Apostrophe plus *s* should be used only for the following:

- **Contractions**—Words from which one or more letters have been dropped, such as *I'll*, *can't*, *you'd*, and *he's*

- **Possessives**—For instance, IBM's new chairman or the company's headquarters

Nonetheless, many people mistakenly use an apostrophe plus *s* in plurals, especially when pluralizing acronyms or numbers, as shown in Figure 8.8. Among people who know and understand this rule, violating it will cost you substantial amounts of credibility. Message: ineffective management.

This error can compound the grammatical mistake by leading to momentary confusion and more work for your audience. Consider the following sentence:

DVD's produce sharper images than VCR's because a DVD's resolution of 500 lines is greater than a VCR's resolution of 240 lines.

The first DVD and VHS references are plural; the second references are possessive.

Using acronyms is risky because they might be unfamiliar to part of your audience. If you do use an acronym, the correct way to turn it into a plural form is with a lowercase *s* and no apostrophe. The same applies to a number or to any other word that needs to be expressed as a plural, as shown in Figure 8.9.

> 66 The use of an apostrophe plus *s* (*'s*) to mark the plural form is simply wrong. 99

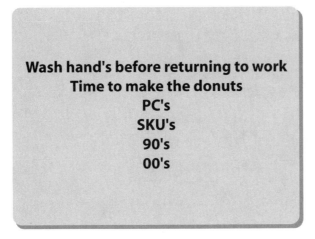

Actually, you can and should avoid using apostrophe plus *s* at all in your presentations. Although it is grammatically correct, you can exercise literary license in the interest of Less Is More. Eliminating apostrophe plus *s* eliminates extra characters, making the text easier to read and faster to comprehend. See the difference between "IBM's New Chairman" and "New IBM Chairman."

Keep Your Font Choices Simple

Most graphics programs, including Microsoft's PowerPoint, provide dozens of type styles, known as *fonts*. Some cost-conscious presenters seem to think, "We've paid for all these fonts, we ought to use all of them." The result is a slide that looks like Figure 8.10.

> 66 You can and should avoid using apostrophe plus *s* at all in your presentations. 99

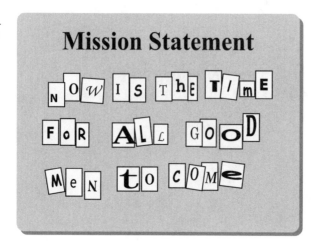

For all your text slides, resist the temptation to get too creative with font choices. Use two or, at most, three different type styles for a single presentation. The result will be a unified look and feel that conveys a clear, consistent message.

One easy way to add creative styling and remain simple is to use one font style for titles and another for bullets; another way is to use two sizes of the same font, a larger one for titles and a smaller one for bullets. You can add further styling by choosing one color for titles and another for bullets, or you can make one of your choices an italic version of the same font. Less Is More is particularly applicable when it comes to typographic choices.

Proportional Spacing

Let's say you've followed the 4 × 4 rule for your bullet slide, and it looks like Figure 8.11.

See the problem? All the bullets are bunched up in the top half of the slide, leaving the bottom half empty. The look is not only unbalanced, but the empty space sets up an anticipation that is not going to be resolved. You can easily remedy this problem with proportional spacing: Distribute the bullets evenly over the entire slide, as in Figure 8.12.

> 66 Use two or, at most, three different type styles for a single presentation. 99

Visual Style

Many business presentations are supported by a collection of slides that are only text—no pictorial, relational, or numeric slides at all. Not only does this border on the Presentation-As-Document Syndrome, but it also looks bland and boring. Twenty all-text slides in a row can produce the MEGO effect.

Furthermore, reading an all-text slide feels like hard work, even when the slide is designed according to the previously mentioned principles. Figure 8.13 is an example.

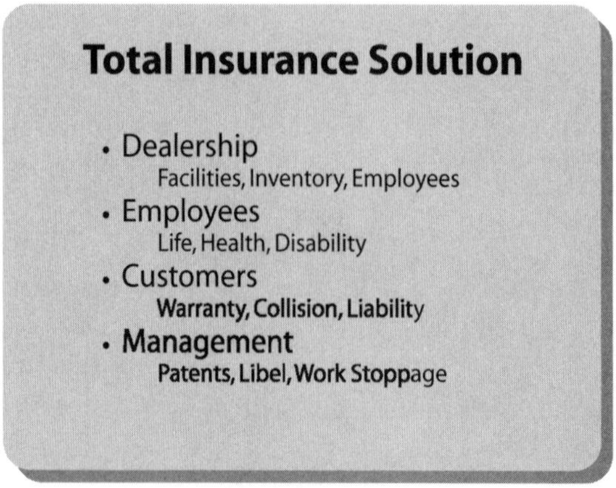

FIGURE 8.13

All-text slide ×
20 = MEGO.

Total Insurance Solution

- Dealership
  Facilities, Inventory, Employees
- Employees
  Life, Health, Disability
- Customers
  Warranty, Collision, Liability
- Management
  Patents, Libel, Work Stoppage

There's nothing "wrong" with this slide, but it's certainly not interesting or even visually appealing.

You can add texture to an all-text slide like this without adding or subtracting a single letter. The secret is to use the simple design tools included in Microsoft PowerPoint. Figure 8.14 shows an example.

FIGURE 8.14

All-text slide +
texture =
audience
interest.

Total Insurance Solution

Dealership	Facilities, Inventory, Employees
Employees	Life, Health, Disability
Customers	Warranty, Collision, Liability
Management	Patents, Libel, Work Stoppage

By putting the text in a table format and judiciously using lines and shading, you can create a much more attractive and interesting version of the slide. It also makes the information easier to read. Grouping related items visually reduces the interpretive work your audience must do to follow the flow of your ideas.

Microsoft PowerPoint provides a wealth of design options for adding texture to your text slides with countless styles, colors, elements, and formats.

You can also create emphasis by using a technique called *reverse out*, which sets off a headline from the rest of your text by reversing the background and font colors, as shown in Figure 8.15.

Black on White

White on Black

You can also enhance the design of the background by adding stripes, borders, edges, and cornices. So many interesting design options are available that you can easily get carried away. For example, one option is gradient shading, as shown in Figure 8.16.

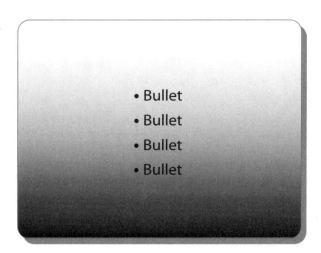

• Bullet

• Bullet

• Bullet

• Bullet

Figure 8.16 looks cool at first, but then you realize that it's difficult to read the last bullet. Not to worry; there's always another bell or whistle in the graphics toolbox. You can add a double gradient (see Figure 8.17).

But now you realize you can't read the first bullet!

FIGURE 8.17

Twice as cool but still unreadable: double-gradient shading.

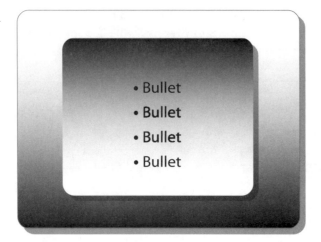

The point here is the same as with font choices: Remember the Less Is More principle. Many presenters get carried away with the plethora of fancy graphic toys available. Choose one or two graphics effects that enhance the clarity and attractiveness of your slide design, and use only these throughout your presentation. Select a limited color palette—two or three colors at most—to complement the colors in your company logo, and use them consistently. For example, if you use a gold border and a royal blue headline on your first slide, every slide should contain a gold border and a royal blue headline.

Finally, optimize all your text slides by following these simple guidelines.

Text Guidelines

- Create a consistent look and feel and maintain it throughout.
- Be consistent in your choice of font, as well as in your choice of case.
- Keep font size to a minimum of 24 or 28 points.
- Avoid abbreviations at all costs.
- Use sharp contrast: light text on a dark background, or vice versa.
- Insert your company logo, but don't make it look like a neon sign; treat it instead as a watermark, with a subtle, embossed effect.
- Avoid the clutter caused by recurring slogans, datelines, copyrights, and the ubiquitous "Company Confidential" warning in the periphery of every single slide.

> 66 Choose one or two graphics effects that enhance the clarity and attractiveness of your slide design, and use only these throughout your presentation. 99

- Use blank space. You don't have to fill every nook and cranny of every slide with information. Newspaper advertisements use white space to set off text. Look at them, see the difference, and follow their example.

You'll notice that I haven't mentioned the differences between serif and sans serif fonts or text justification right, left, or center. These typographic fine points are matters of individual taste, and as the Latin proverb tells us, *De gustibus non est disputandum* (there's no arguing taste).

Follow the previous guidelines, and your text graphics will be simple, consistent, and logical, reinforcing the subliminal message of effective management.

In the next chapter, you'll see how the same basic principles that create winning text graphics also apply to numeric graphics.

THE ABSOLUTE MINIMUM

- Minimize the eye sweeps by restricting the bullet text to a single line.
- Choose one or two graphics effects that enhance the clarity and attractiveness of your slide design, and use only these throughout your presentation.

9

MAKING THE NUMBERS SING

Numbers play a key role in any business presentation. Revenues, units shipped, profits, and market share are the hits, runs, and errors of the business scorecard, and everyone in business understands their importance.

This is not to say that everyone in business feels equally at home when it comes to interpreting numbers. There are the green-eyeshade types who immediately recognize key trends and can quickly pick out the most important item in a column of figures. Then there are the rest of us, who need a little time and a lot of context to fully grasp the meaning of a profit and loss statement or balance sheet.

The Power of Numeric Graphics

When you're in a persuasive situation, you want to win the agreement of both the number-savvy and the number-shy. Skillfully designed numeric graphics can help achieve that. They translate digits and decimals into visual images that make abstract relationships concrete and much easier to recognize.

> 66 When you're in a persuasive situation, you want to win the agreement of both the number-savvy and the number-shy. 99

Unfortunately, many of the numeric graphics used in presentations serve to obscure rather than clarify the facts. All too often, the graphics are sheer data dumps loaded with needless information, are poorly organized, and are visually cluttered. Such numeric slides take a long time to explain and even longer for the audience to understand. Often, the audience members decide that such slides aren't worth the effort and give up. Many an important presentation gets derailed this way.

This needn't happen with your presentations. The same basic principles you learned to apply to your entire presentation—presenter focus, Less Is More, and minimize eye sweeps—also apply to numeric graphics. Let them be your guidelines to creating clear and effective images that drive your story home and reinforce your key ideas.

Bar Charts

Let's begin with the Problem/Solution approach by looking at an all-too-typical numeric slide, the bar chart shown in Figure 9.1. You've probably encountered this type of graphic in many presentations. This example depicts six years of steady sales growth in the history of an up-and-coming company, information that ought to play an exciting role in telling the company's story.

FIGURE 9.1

How *not* to design a bar chart.

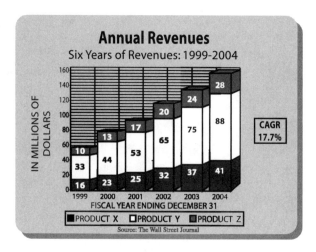

There's certainly plenty of information here. Of course, the problem is that there's too much information for a presentation. If this chart was in a document, such as a business plan or an annual report, the reader might need all this data to understand the writer's point. The reader would also have close-up access to the document. But in a presentation, the audience is forced involuntarily to make multiple eye sweeps across the enlarged image to see all the data, while their minds are simultaneously processing all the data. All this ratcheting around and thinking is excessive sensory activity that disconnects the audience from the presenter. The slide becomes the focus of the presentation, drastically reducing the potential to persuade.

> 66 The same basic principles you learned to apply to your entire presentation—presenter focus, Less Is More, and minimize eye sweeps—also apply to numeric graphics. 99

Let's think about what's wrong here: First of all, notice how much print clutters the slide. There's a title and a subtitle that essentially repeat the same information. There are two labels, one at the left side of the slide ("In Millions Of Dollars") that is standing on its end and one sprawled out along the bottom of the slide ("Fiscal Year Ending December 31"). Each label takes up a great deal of space while providing information that is either very simple or not terribly important. More than 30 numbers are on the slide: 9 along the left scale, 18 superimposed on the 6 bars, and the 6 dates along the bottom edge of the graph. The CAGR (Compound Annual Growth Rate) sticks out to the right like an outrigger. The source credit to *The Wall Street Journal* is in a font size so tiny it rings of the fine print in a shady contract. The 6 bars depicting revenues are each subdivided into 3 different colored sections. And all this data is backed by grid lines that resemble bargain-basement, bamboo-slat Venetian blinds.

Clearly, the person who designed this slide has never heard of Less Is More, or didn't believe it.

Notice how much work your eyes (and your mind) must do to absorb all this information. It's not only a matter of wading through all the words and numbers to decipher which ones are important and which aren't, but it's also a matter of attempting to draw connections among the disjointed parts of the graph. In short, this slide is a visual mess. How can we improve it?

We can start by simplifying and cleaning up the unnecessary verbiage. Because the title and subtitle are redundant, we can eliminate the subtitle. The graph itself clearly contains six bars, which are labeled by year, so it isn't necessary for the subtitle to spell out the number of years covered.

Rather than devoting so much space to the labels "In Millions Of Dollars" and "Fiscal Year Ending December 31," we can use simple abbreviations. Nor do we need to spell out full dates; in this context, if a bar is labeled "'99," everyone in the audience will understand that it represents 1999 rather than 1899 or 2099. Give *The Wall Street Journal* its due by making the font size legible. Finally, does your audience really need to know the exact dollar figure for each product sold? Probably not; it depends on the point of the slide. If the purpose is to demonstrate total revenue growth, the audience can see the relative amounts of each product by the colors. Remove the numbers in the bars.

This is a distinct improvement. We've substantially reduced the amount of work the audience must do to understand the graph. But there's still more to be done. To identify the various colored parts of the bars, the audience members must shift their eyes up and down repeatedly to the legend at the bottom, like a bouncing yo-yo.

Only when the audience discovers the legend at the bottom of the slide, which matches the colors to Product X, Product Y, and Product Z, does the explanation become clear. You can feel the movement here on the page, where the distance is only several inches. Imagine the feeling when you traverse a space of several feet on a projection screen. Minimize eye sweeps.

Furthermore, anyone in the audience who wants to figure out the value of a particular bar must move her eyes back and forth, left and right, several times between the scale and the bar, like a fast and furious Ping-Pong match—a futile match, too, because at a distance, the human eye can't find the exact tick mark. Again, minimize eye sweeps.

We can make some simple adjustments to clear up these problems. Look at Figure 9.2.

FIGURE 9.2

The same bar chart, simplified and clarified.

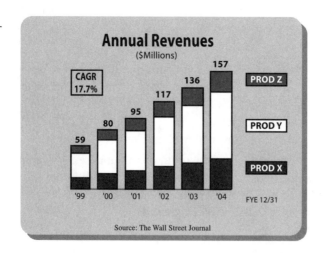

By removing the scale from the left and placing the revenue totals directly on top of the bars, we see the growth trend in one sweep of the eyes. By removing the legend at the bottom of the graph (along with the usual trifling little squares) and simply labeling the three bar segments with colored text boxes along the right margin, the eyes identify products X, Y, and Z at the end of the eye sweep.

> 66 Any numeric slide can be dramatically improved by ruthlessly eliminating unnecessary words, numbers, scales, legends, and effects. 99

Simpler still would be to eliminate the stacks and create separate charts for each product.

Notice the 3D effect on the bars in Figure 9.1. Some people like this effect, and others hate it, but it's really not a question of taste. Instead, the question should be, "Does it add anything to the display of information in the graph?" The answer is "no." There's nothing 3D about the annual revenues, so making the bars 3D is only window dressing. In fact, by introducing more lines, shapes, and colors, a 3D effect has the potential to confuse the audience about what's really important in the graph. Remember, Less Is More.

The simplified version of the slide will have much more impact in your presentation. The important story it tells about your company's impressive sales growth will hit home much more forcefully. Any numeric slide can be dramatically improved by ruthlessly eliminating unnecessary words, numbers, scales, legends, and effects.

Pie Charts

Figure 9.3 shows a typical pie chart (also called a *circle chart*). This kind of chart is useful for showing a total amount divided into subordinate parts; in this case, the chart shows how a company's sales are divided geographically. At a glance, you can easily see the relative share of the whole that each part, or each wedge of pie, represents.

Unfortunately, the chart is needlessly cluttered and confusing to read. Stacking the name of the sales region, the sales figure, and the percentage (for example, "Europe," "$11 Million," and "22%") forces the viewer to pause and sort out what each element means.

Now look at the version in Figure 9.4.

FIGURE 9.3
A typical pie
chart.

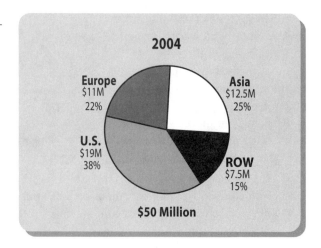

FIGURE 9.4
The same chart,
simplified.

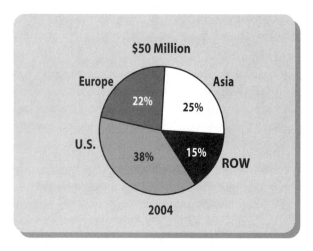

The geographic labels remain outside the pie, but the percentages are now inside the wedges. This arrangement is clearer because text usually takes up more space than numbers. If any wedge is too small to contain its number, use a callout—that is, place the number just outside the wedge with a fine line to indicate where it belongs.

Notice how separating the label from the number makes both much easier to read. Notice, too, that we have omitted the specific dollar figures shown in the first version of the graph. In a pie chart, the relative size of each wedge is the most important information.

> **❝** In a pie chart, the relative size of each wedge is the most important information. **❞**

Finally, note that we've shifted the date to the bottom of the pie. That's where the timeline appears in most business charts.

Follow these general guidelines when you create a pie chart and your audience will be able to easily read and understand it.

Typography in Numeric Graphics

The axis label on the left side of Figure 9.5 is stacked. Type set this way is very hard to read. Think about it: The stacked label, containing eight letters, causes your eyes to make seven carriage returns. Ouch!

FIGURE 9.5

Seven carriage returns: a stacked axis label.

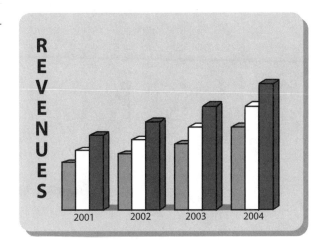

A close cousin of the stacked vertical label is the vertical label on end, as shown in Figure 9.6.

FIGURE 9.6

Ears on shoulders: a rotated axis label.

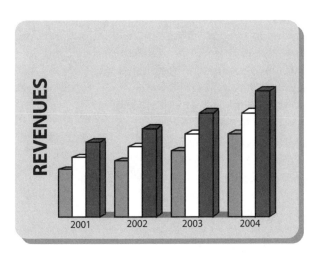

This practice is a carryover from documents. In a document, the reader can rotate the document to read the word *Revenues*. In a projected presentation slide, however, the audience members are forced to rotate their heads. This often seems like an adult variation of Simple Simon: "Left ears on left shoulders, please!"

These problems are easy to solve, as shown in Figure 9.7.

FIGURE 9.7

No head movement: a much-more-legible horizontal label.

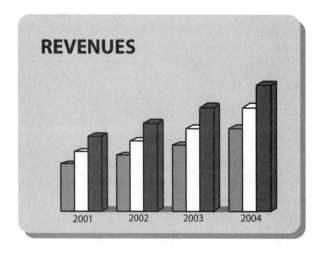

Use a horizontal label like the one in Figure 9.7, which makes the chart much clearer and easier to read.

The Hockey Stick

Another example of conditioned eye movement is the way audiences perceive and react to information. Through long experience with graphs and charts, business-people are accustomed to responding to what is known as the *hockey stick*, which expresses positive results moving upward to the right. A trend sloping in the downward direction implies negative results and is therefore a counterintuitive movement. Unfortunately, many presenters, as well as many professional graphic artists, design their bar charts counter to these psychological implications.

Figure 9.8 is a reproduction of an actual newspaper advertisement, doctored slightly to protect the guilty (we've used the fictitious bank name "Comet").

> 66 ...businesspeople are accustomed to responding to what is known as the hockey stick, which expresses positive results moving upward to the right. 99

FIGURE 9.8

The reverse
hockey stick,
going downward.

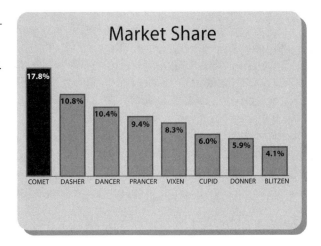

Comet wanted to brag about its leading market share over all its competitors in corporate debt underwriting. Although Comet was proud of its achievement, its advertising designers set up the bars with movement downward rather than upward,
counterintuitive to positive results.

Figure 9.9 shows how Comet's ad should have been depicted, with the bars implying
movement upward and to the right. The hockey stick now expresses rising action.
Furthermore, the bars end with Comet's name. By placing your company name at
the final climactic point, you tacitly take a superior position and it becomes the last
word your audience will see and remember.

FIGURE 9.9

The natural
hockey stick,
upward and to
the right.

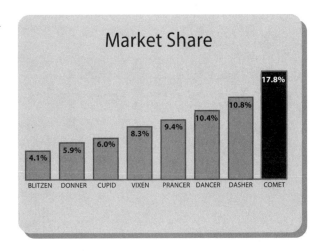

Subtle? Yes, But...

The stylistic points presented in this chapter might strike you as picky. "Oh, come on," you might say. "The members of my audience aren't graphic artists or designers. Will anyone really notice if I arrange the bars in the graph in reverse order or stack the letters in the vertical label?"

> 66 You can't afford to over-look any factor that might influence your audience, no matter how subtle it might appear. 99

Maybe not consciously. But our cultural conditioning to react to visual cues is very deep and powerful; so much so that, even when your audiences don't consciously recognize such design flaws, they respond to them with a sense of unease, uncertainty, or dislike. They might not realize what's bothering them. At most, they might think, "Those slides look a little odd," or "There's something here that's not quite right."

Is this a serious problem? It can be. Remember, chances are good that your persuasive effort will be competing against powerful opposing forces, ranging from your direct competitors to the subtler forces of indifference, apathy, and inattention. It's easy for anyone to doubt your expertise, to question your motives, to be distracted, or simply to lose interest. You can't afford to overlook any factor that might influence your audience, no matter how subtle it might appear.

Persuading your audience to respond to your call to action is almost always an uphill battle. Why make it harder, even 10% harder, by designing graphics that work against your message? Make your graphics work for you.

THE ABSOLUTE MINIMUM

■ Any numeric slide can be dramatically improved by ruthlessly eliminating unnecessary words, numbers, scales, legends, and effects.

10

USING GRAPHICS TO HELP YOUR STORY FLOW

In the last two chapters, we focused on designing slides that convey information clearly and effectively. You've absorbed many details about everything from font styles to graph labels. Now it's time to take a step back and return to one of the earlier concepts in this book: specifically, flow.

The 35,000-Foot Overview

Every communications medium has its own techniques for helping its audience remain oriented and follow the flow. Think about text, where the reader is the audience to the writer. In a book, a magazine, a newspaper, or a printed report, the designers and editors provide the reader with many tools to help track the writer's flow: the table of contents, the index, and the running heads along the top or bottom of the page. Even more important, the reader has the luxury of random access to the writer's material. The reader can navigate through the text independently by visiting and revisiting the table of contents or the index or by flipping backward and forward as often as needed to follow the overall flow. Think of Russian novels, where all those multiple names and nicknames of the characters are listed up front. Think of plays, where the dramatis personae, or cast of characters, precedes the first scene. Through long practice, readers are accustomed to steering through the structure of written texts on their own.

> 66 In a presentation, the audience can access the presenter's material only in a linear fashion: one slide at a time, one spoken sentence at a time, and all this under the presenter's control. 99

Presentations are different. In a presentation, the audience can access the presenter's material only in a linear fashion: one slide at a time, one spoken sentence at a time, and all this under the presenter's control. After a slide disappears from the screen, it's gone forever. The audience doesn't have the opportunity to flip back and forth at will to clarify the presentation's flow.

Just as in the telling of the presentation story, the audience receives the visual content at the level of the trees. And, just as in the telling of the story, the presenter's job is to rise up from the trees and give the audience a view of the entire forest. As always, the presenter's job is to navigate the audience's minds, but now the presenter can also navigate the audience's eyes.

The Flow Structures in Chapter 5, "Plotting Your Story: Flow Structures," and telling 'em what you're gonna tell 'em in Chapter 6, "Starting Your Story: Capturing Your Audience Immediately," can help your audience follow your flow, but both of these are purely verbal techniques. Graphics can help express flow, too. You can design your slides to convey the connections among your ideas. You can use a set of simple visual tools to create continuity and help your audience track the overall logic of your presentation.

note I provide my clients with a paper version of the storyboard. The Microsoft PowerPoint version of this aspect is called Slide Sorter View. Both options provide a panoramic view of your story.

Before introducing these tools, however, it's important to step back and check the flow of your presentation, to examine it as a whole, by taking a 35,000-foot overview. One valuable tool to do this is the storyboard form, illustrated in Figure 10.1.

FIGURE 10.1

The storyboard form.

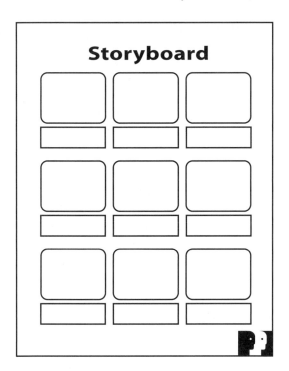

Television and film directors use storyboards to plan their end products, whether it is a 60-second commercial or a multimillion-dollar special-effects epic. They map out the camera angles of each scene and then envision how the individual scenes will combine into a whole sequence.

This view lets you see all the slides for a given presentation at a glance, a perspective that minimizes your focus on details and offers a broader outlook of the landscape. It's an efficient planning tool that helps you check the progression of your story. Note that there is also a small rectangular box beneath each slide image where you can enter notes on your narrative, further clarifying your flow.

Figure 10.2 illustrates how the panoramic view works. Look at your slides in the storyboard form. See them in groups, reflecting the Flow Structure you chose for your presentation. In this example, the presentation includes four parts: an Introduction, an Opportunity section, a Leverage section, and the Conclusion. Each section is supported by a group of slides. Within each section, every slide should fit logically into place.

> 66 Look at your slides in the storyboard form. 99

FIGURE 10.2

A panoramic view.

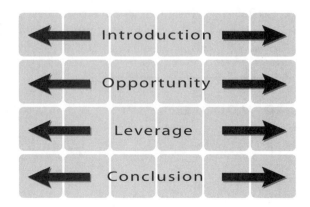

When you scan slides in this view, it should become evident when some slides don't fit where you've placed them. You might want to shift them to a different part of the sequence, or they might be extraneous, in which case, you might want to eliminate them altogether. The connection between any one part of the presentation and the next should also be clear. If it isn't, you might want to rethink your sequence. You could add, delete, or shuffle slides so the logic is evident, or you might even try a different Flow Structure.

The ultimate technique for checking your flow is to read only the titles of your slides, as in Figure 10.3. If you can trace the logic of your entire presentation by reading these few words, bypassing the bullets, graphs, or other content, you've created clarity. A presentation that achieves this makes it easy for your audience to follow and easy for you to deliver.

FIGURE 10.3

The ultimate flow check.

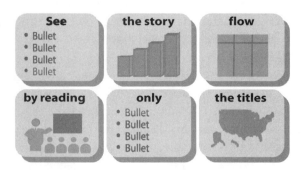

Graphic Continuity Techniques

After your verbal logic is clear, you can turn to graphics to help communicate your flow. Well-designed graphics not only convey information clearly and attractively, but also help establish the connections among ideas. Again, the panoramic view offers an excellent perspective on the flow of your presentation. If the continuity of your graphics is not apparent, it might look like Figure 10.4.

Try to scan this storyboard from slide to slide. Because no two slides look alike, the presentation begins anew with each slide, forcing you to adjust repeatedly to new content, new form, and a new look. Now think of your audience. Without the luxury of the panoramic view, they will see only one new slide at a time. They will be forced to work even harder to adjust to each new content, new form, and new look. By the end of the presentation, they will be exhausted and, most likely, confused. Don't make them think!

> **tip**
>
> In Microsoft PowerPoint, you can use either the Slide Sorter or the Outline view to read only the titles.

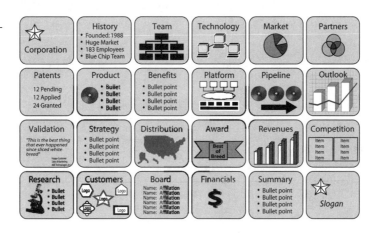

FIGURE 10.4
No two slides alike.

Fortunately, you can use a number of proven graphics techniques to help express the flow of your presentation in your slides. Let's look at these techniques, along with illustrative examples drawn from actual business presentations.

Bumper Slides

The first continuity technique, and the simplest, is the bumper slide. This technique is drawn from the field of publishing. Look at any lengthy nonfiction book. You're likely to find that it is divided into chapters and parts, and most often find that each part is separated from the next part by a full page containing only the part number and a title.

> 66 The ultimate technique for checking your flow is to read only the titles of your slides. 99

> 66 Well-designed graphics not only convey information clearly and attractively, but also help establish the connections among ideas. 99

The purpose: closure of the outbound section and a lead in to the inbound section. The advantage: The reader's mind is cleared of the last subject and primed for the next. In a presentation, the bumper slide signals a transition to a new section. Think of the bumper slide as the sorbet that is served between courses of a fine meal to cleanse the palate.

Figure 10.5 shows the simplest and most effective form of the bumper slide. It contains a single line of text (remember: minimize eye sweeps by avoiding wordwrap). That one line previews the contents of the next section of the presentation. For example, you might have bumper slides reading "Market Opportunity," "Unique Technology," "Industry Leadership," and "Business Results," each of which would serve to introduce a set of ensuing slides covering each of these topics.

> **tip**
>
> A simple image or symbol works great as a bumper slide. It could be your company logo, an image relevant to the theme of your presentation, or an icon that suggests the content of the subsequent portion of the presentation.

FIGURE 10.5

Bumper slide: notice the centered text.

To differentiate the bumper slide from all the other slides, center the text both horizontally (left to right) and vertically (top to bottom).

You can also use your agenda as a bumper slide (see Figure 10.6) and, with it, track the overall outline of your presentation. For this approach, each bumper slide displays the complete agenda with the upcoming item highlighted, as opposed to dimmed, which causes your audience to squint.

> **caution**
>
> Use the progressive agenda approach only with longer presentations, say 30 minutes or more. In shorter presentations, if you reprise your agenda after just one or two slides, your audience will feel patronized. They might say to themselves, "I got it! You don't have to remind me!"

The bumper slide tells your audience exactly where they are in the presentation, as well as where they've been and where they're going. Think of this as a progressive agenda.

66 In shorter presentations, if you reprise your agenda after just one or two slides, your audience will feel patronized. **99**

FIGURE 10.6
Bumper slide: It's got an agenda.

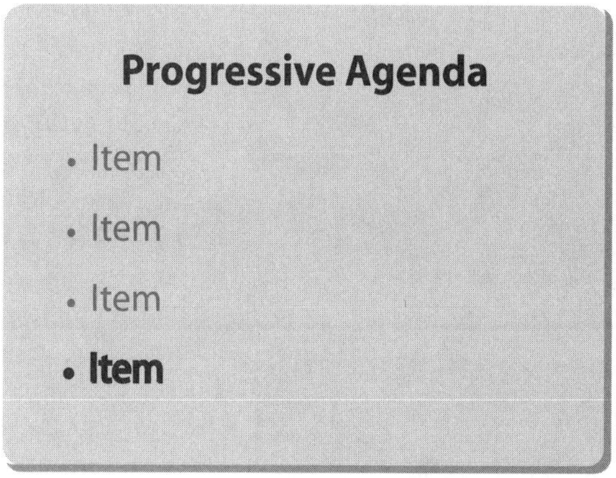

Progressive Agenda

- Item
- Item
- Item
- **Item**

In longer and more complicated presentations, your audience will appreciate these milestones. Here's a case study from the world of biotechnology.

CASE STUDY: GETTING UNDER THE SKIN OF A COMPLEX TOPIC

In 1999, Dr. Jacques Essinger, the CEO of Modex Therapeutics (a Swiss biotech company focused on cell therapy), engaged me to help him and his team develop their IPO roadshow. The company went public the following year on Switzerland's equivalent of the NASDAQ, the Nouveau Marche (SWXNM), and performed very well.

But in mid-2001, the biotech sector in general—and growth companies like Modex in particular—fell out of favor with investors, and Modex's share price dropped. Jacques formulated a new strategy to acquire additional related technologies that could produce more revenues. When the acquisitions were done, Jacques called on me to help him prepare a new presentation to announce the new strategy to the Swiss financial community.

Because the focus of this chapter is graphic continuity, I'll discuss only the heart of Jacques's presentation, where he wanted to describe his newly expanded core business to his potential new investors, none of whom was a biotech scientist.

Jacques had a very crisp and strong opening sequence at the front end and two brief sections on strategy and finance at the back end, but the core of his presentation was an

continues

FIGURE 10.7
The Modex bumper slide, setting the scene.

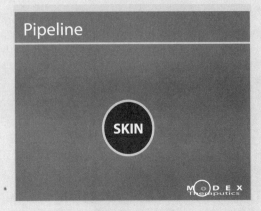

exemplary illustration of the use of bumper slides. He started by identifying Modex's original and continuing focus on skin with a simple circle, as shown in Figure 10.7.

Then, using the Microsoft PowerPoint animation feature, he sprouted three smaller circles out from the main circle, as in Figure 10.8. The movement of the smaller circles expressed the broadening of Modex's original business model from skin to related indications. This graphic expansion thematically represented opening a pipeline to potential new revenue sources. This bumper slide also established the agenda for the material to follow.

FIGURE 10.8
The Modex bumper slide, setting the agenda.

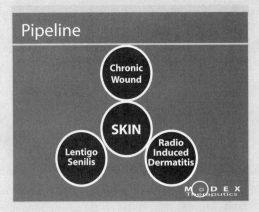

In his narration, Jacques described how he planned to cover each of the skin indications in the same order. If this sounds familiar, it is a composite of the Form/Function and Parallel Tracks Flow Structures, expressed graphically.

Then, using highlighting, Jacques moved into the first indication, chronic wound (see Figure 10.9).

FIGURE 10.9
The Modex bumper slide, first topic area.

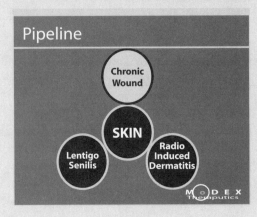

Jacques then drilled down into the chronic wound topic for a total of 19 slides, most of them as simply constructed as the bumper slide. For instance, he used a pyramid to describe the various layers of the market. The pyramid appeared in a 6-slide sequence and again later within the segment as a 3-slide sequence. Of the slides, 2 were pictures, 2 were bar charts, and 2 were boxes with

continues

minimal text laid out to indicate related information. Only 4 of the 19 slides in this entire sequence were text. This was certainly not a Presentation-As-Document.

Now Jacques was ready to shift to the radio induced dermatitis topic, and he did this by returning to his bumper slide and shifting the highlighting to the new circle, as shown in Figure 10.10.

FIGURE 10.10

The Modex bumper slide, second topic area.

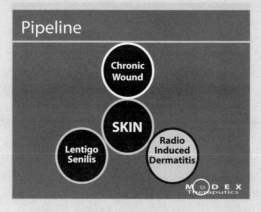

He covered the radio induced dermatitis topic in a five-slide sequence. Then he came back out to his bumper slide and shifted the highlighting to the last indication, lentigo senilis, as shown in Figure 10.11.

Note that a sufficient number of slides appears between bumper slides to warrant their repetitive use without appearing patronizing.

Jacques covered lentigo senilis in another five-slide sequence, two of which were pictures and three of which were text. By then, he was done with his core business and ready to move into the home stretch of the presentation.

Although Modex's story is a complex one with many supporting details, Jacques's use of consistent graphics, linked and united by bumper slides, made the story clear and easy to follow.

FIGURE 10.11

The Modex bumper slide, third topic area.

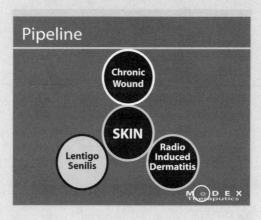

Indexing/Color Coding

Indexing/color coding is another graphic continuity technique to navigate through longer presentations. Whereas the bumper slide appears intermittently, indexing uses a recurring object that is highlighted with different colors or shades coded to map the different sections of your presentation. This approach helps your audience track your flow with a minimum of effort on their part, as well as yours.

This technique is often used in extensive technical presentations that have multiple sections, each of which is covered in deep, granular detail. The best way to portray this technique is with the simple example of a four-part strategy, depicted in Figure 10.12.

As shown in Figure 10.12, this company's four-part business strategy is represented by a circular pie icon divided into four different-colored wedges. If you were the presenter, you would show this slide near the start of your presentation to describe and discuss your overall strategy. When focusing on the first strategic element (Strategy A), you would shift the pie icon to the upper-left corner and highlight one wedge, using its signature color, as shown in Figure 10.13. You would then add details about this part of the strategy in the bullets. As a result, the pie becomes clearly identifiable as an index.

> 66 Whereas the bumper slide appears intermittently, indexing uses a recurring object that is highlighted with different colors or shades coded to map the different sections of your presentation. 99

FIGURE 10.12

Index/color coding for a four-part business strategy.

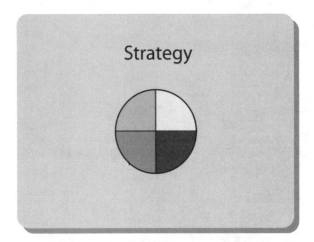

FIGURE 10.13

Strategy, part one: Note the icon in the corner.

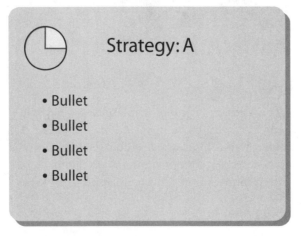

The next slide moves on to the second part of the strategy (see Figure 10.14). The highlight in the index shifts to the second pie wedge and its signature color. The explanatory bullets change, providing discussion points to elaborate.

FIGURE 10.14

Strategy, part two.

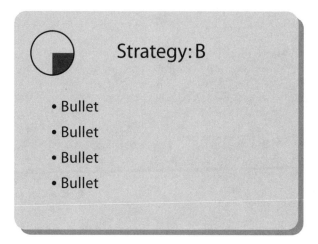

You can already anticipate the progression of the next two slides. The highlight shifts to each of the next two wedges in turn, coming around the horn to complete the circuit. Using the indexing/color coding scheme makes it easy for your audience to stay with your flow. It also creates the subtle, subliminal psychological dynamic of raising expectations and meeting them. Your audience knows that the third and fourth pie wedges will soon be appearing on the screen, and when the color shifts, exactly as they expected, they feel a sense of resolution and satisfaction.

Now let's jump ahead to the end of the circuit where, in Figure 10.15, all four parts of the strategy are reprised in the large pie with all the colors at their full original values. With this slide, you could summarize the strategy and then, by extending the pie with a ring, go on to describe future strategic directions, thus adding value.

This sequence of slides serves as a series of guideposts, visually supporting your narrative as you navigate through all the stages of your presentation and lead your audience to your conclusion.

Icons

Another graphic continuity technique is icons. These are symbols that express relationships among the ideas of your presentation. Icons indicate these connections in a shorthand form your audience can grasp quickly and intuitively. Because

> " Icons indicate these connections in a shorthand form your audience can grasp quickly and intuitively. "

icons are pictorial, they meet the Less Is More criterion by default. Icons also provide relief from the Presentation-As-Document Syndrome with its extended series of text-only slides. Well-chosen icons make an excellent presentation tool.

FIGURE 10.15

Strategy completed, recapped, and extended.

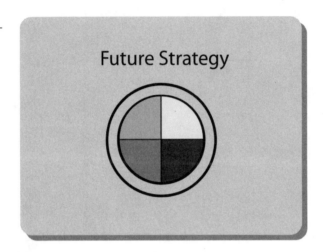

Figure 10.16 shows some classic icons and how you might use them to help illustrate the content of your presentation. We'll discuss them in clockwise order, starting at the top.

In Chinese cosmology, yin and yang are the dual, contrasting forces whose combination gives rise to everything that exists in the universe. For Western audiences, the yin/yang icon simply means "two-part harmony." You might use a version of this icon in a presentation whose theme is the integration of two forces: for example, when explaining the benefits of a merger between two companies or when presenting your firm's two product lines and the complementary benefits they offer.

Many people subscribe to what is commonly known as the *rule of threes*, in the theory that three is an easy amount to remember. If your story contains three key elements, you can pick one of a variety of triplex icons to express them: the triangle, the trident, the three-legged stool, three interlocking arrows, or the three-ring icon.

This image represents harmony among three items. You might use a version of this icon when describing how three forces, groups, or units work together or combine in some way. For example, you could use it when presenting the story of a company that serves three distinct but overlapping markets or customer groups, such as businesses, government, and schools, or when describing a company's three-pronged competitive strategy. If you choose this icon, be sure to set the two rings at the bottom, creating a stable image.

FIGURE 10.16

Strategy, part
two.

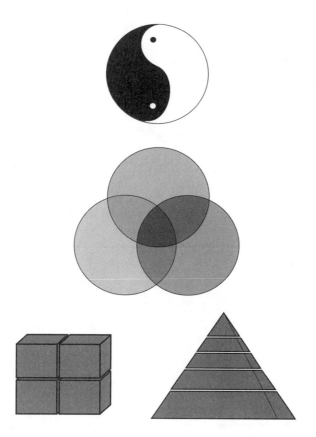

If your story contains four key elements, try the divided cube icon, which suggests four-part harmony. You might use this in a presentation to describe four complementary products, four departments that work together (Sales, Marketing, Info Tech, and Customer Service), four elements in a strategic plan, or four markets in which a company operates (North America, South America, Asia, and Europe).

Finally, the pyramidal icon suggests a set of hierarchical relationships. It could represent layers of management in an organization; an array of products ranging from those that are low-priced and mass-marketed (the bottom layer of the pyramid) to those that are high-priced and sold through specialty outlets (the top of the pyramid); or a sequence of concepts that build on a broad foundation and then on one another, culminating in the most advanced concept.

You saw how I used a pyramid to express a Spatial Flow Structure in Chapter 5 (refer to Figure 5.1). In my own presentations and workshops programs, I describe the components of an effective presentation by starting with a solid story at the foundation and then build up to the top with how to answer questions arising from that story. You can probably think of dozens of other icons you've encountered, each with its own visual statement. If an icon captures and expresses the relationships among your ideas, consider using it throughout your presentation as a visual symbol for your audience.

> 66 If an icon captures and expresses the relationships among your ideas, consider using it throughout your presentation as a visual symbol for your audience. 99

FIGURE 10.17
Cisco Systems' lexicon of icons.

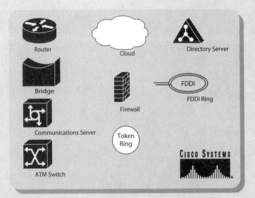

GRAPHICALLY INCREASING COMPREHENSION AT CISCO

Some companies, like Cisco, devote considerable effort to creating icons. Given its complex technology, Cisco endeavors to make comprehension easier for its audiences by expressing that technology in images rather than text. A picture is worth a thousand words.

When Cisco launches a new product family, it carefully creates a specific graphic image to represent that family. The company expends even more effort to develop conceptual graphic images that represent industry-wide functions and processes. These conceptual icons are so important that Cisco has established a set of specific guidelines for their creation.

Gary Stewart has been a technical illustrator for Cisco since 1991 and has overseen the creation of icons that represent such universal networking technology elements as the router, ATM switch, network cloud, firewall, bridge, communication server, and directory server, all shown in Figure 10.17.

Over the years, Cisco has accumulated a full lexicon of icons it uses in its presentations and literature. Cisco also makes these icons available on a public domain site (search for `icons` at `www.cisco.com`); as a result, the symbols have become industry nomenclature as well as an enormous branding initiative for Cisco.

Anchor Objects

The next technique is called anchor objects in which a recurring image appears in a succession of slides to express a continuing relationship. Whereas index/color coding creates continuity with a recurring icon, such as a pie or pyramid, the anchor object option creates continuity with a recurring image that is an integral part of the illustration. This image or object can be a photograph, a sketch, a map, an icon, a screenshot, a logo, or clipart.

> 66 Whereas index/color coding creates continuity with a recurring icon, such as a pie or pyramid, the anchor object option creates continuity with a recurring image that is an integral part of the illustration. 99

Here, you begin a series of slides in which the first in the series contains the anchor object. In the next slide, this object remains in place and is joined by another object, establishing a relationship between the two objects. In the next slide in the series, the two objects remain anchored in place while still another object appears to join them. This visual succession expresses relationships among the objects and provides your audience with continuity.

Figure 10.18 shows how this works.

FIGURE 10.18

Anchor object progression.

As you bring in new objects to join the anchor, you can also create emphasis by highlighting with different colors or shading or by adding borders. Another way to create emphasis is by enlarging any one object as a callout or by adding depth with foreground or background elements. This next example will illustrate.

In Chapter 4, "Finding Your Story: Creative Brainstorming," you met Dr. Robert Colwell, one of the leaders of the engineering team that developed Intel's next-generation integrated circuit, the P6. For the launch presentation at a technical symposium, Bob used a schematic diagram of the new chip in very basic black and white as the anchor object to track the flow of his presentation.

In the slides that follow (Figures 10.19–10.23), each slide is a visual variation on the one before. Building on the schematic diagram, Bob highlighted some of the objects by reversing the black and white, thus shifting the audience's focus from one element of the chip's design to another. As Bob navigated through his presentation, he also used enlarged callouts in the foreground.

FIGURE 10.19

Intel uses the bus diagram of a new chip design as an anchor object.

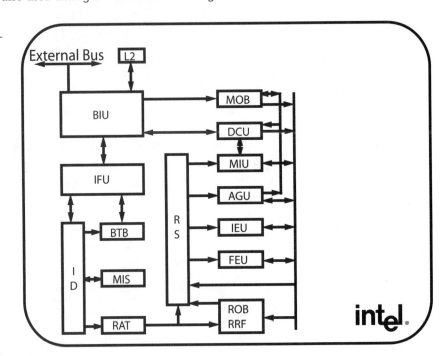

FIGURE 10.20

Part of the anchor object is highlighted for emphasis.

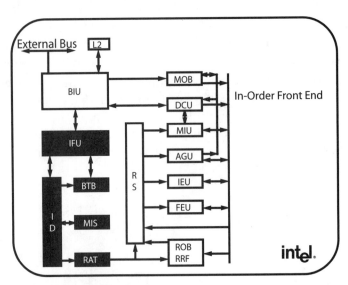

FIGURE 10.21

Part of the anchor object is enlarged for emphasis.

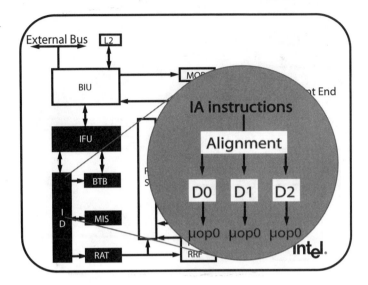

FIGURE 10.22

The highlighting is shifted.

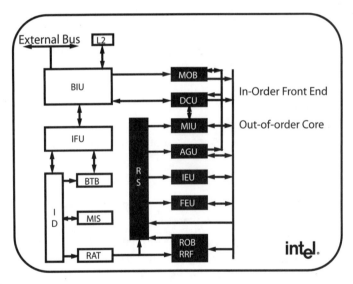

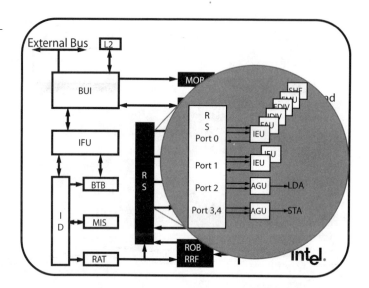

This simple graphical design provided a clear roadmap for a highly technical narrative. By the end of Bob Colwell's presentation, the audience of his peers not only had a clear understanding of all the key features of the new Intel chip design, but had also gained a healthy respect for Bob and for Intel.

Remember Bob's post-mortem: "I didn't get any of the hardball questions I was worried about. I wonder if maybe potential hostile questioners were holding back, for fear of 'losing' the argument to somebody who appeared to have done his homework and seemed thoroughly in control of the proceedings."

Anticipation Space

The final graphic continuity technique is drawn from the cinema, and it's called anticipation space. Here's how it works.

Imagine you're watching a film. In one particular scene, one of the characters is seen in close-up, his face virtually filling the screen. After a moment, the camera widens out slowly, leaving the character in the left corner of the screen. While the character remains visible, you can now see the background. The setting is a cafe, and the character is sitting alone at a table in a cafe. What would you anticipate?

When I ask my clients this question, they invariably respond, "Someone or something is going to enter the scene." And when I ask why, they say, "To fill the empty space on the right side."

Of course, they're correct. Years of watching movies and television have conditioned us to recognize that when an empty space is opened up on the screen, that space is going to be filled. In our imagined movie scene, the man's lover would appear and take the seat across the cafe table from him.

The same sense of audience anticipation can be created using simple graphics in a business presentation. Look at Figure 10.24.

FIGURE 10.24

Anticipation space.

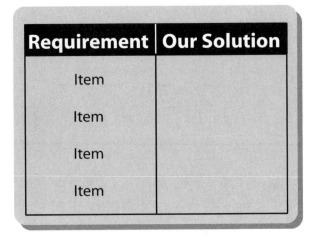

Requirement	Our Solution
Item	
Item	
Item	
Item	

What do you anticipate when you look at this slide? Of course, you expect the empty space on the right side of the slide to be filled. More specifically, you expect four items to appear, corresponding to the four items on the left side. Four is the only possible number. Three items would disappoint you; five would confuse you.

The only possible slide to follow Figure 10.24 is the one in Figure 10.25. This slide answers our questions, satisfies our expectations, and fulfills our anticipation. The subliminal message: Our company promises, and it delivers.

FIGURE 10.25

Anticipation fulfilled.

Requirement	Our Solution
Item	Item
Item	Item
Item	Item
Item	Item

Anticipation space is a simple but visually powerful technique and is another instance of subliminally managing your audience's minds.

Here's how one company used anticipation space to illustrate an Issues/Actions/Matrix/Parallel Tracks Flow Structure: The company had faltered and was attempting a turnaround. It brought in a new management team that decided to reposition the entire business model. They called on me to help them develop a presentation to describe the turnaround strategy to their employees, investors, and other concerned stakeholders.

The new team identified five factors they had to address to reposition the company. For their first slide (see Figure 10.26), they designed a matrix that listed the five factors on one side, leaving corresponding blank spaces on the other side for the actions they planned to take, setting up the anticipation.

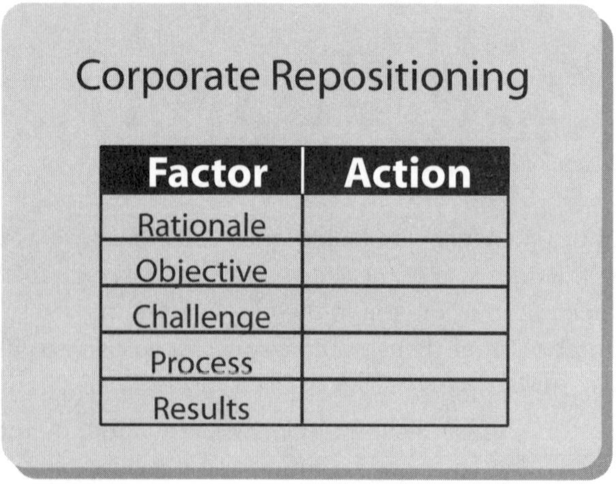

FIGURE 10.26

Anticipation space with the Matrix/Parallel Tracks Flow Structure.

In the next slide they filled the empty spaces with an action for each factor (see Figure 10.27). Thus, the anticipation was resolved.

Using the same format, they continued on to another slide to discuss their corporate identity. They listed the factors they had to address on the left and then filled in the spaces on the right with actions they intended to take. On a third slide, following the same parallel track, they used the same format again to discuss their product positioning. Again, they listed the factors on the left and filled the spaces on the right with the actions they intended to take.

Those three slides—flanked by an opening title slide and a closing title slide—served as the basis for their entire presentation (see Figure 10.28).

FIGURE 10.27

The same matrix, with the anticipation space filled in.

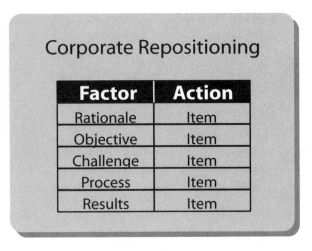

FIGURE 10.28

The entire presentation.

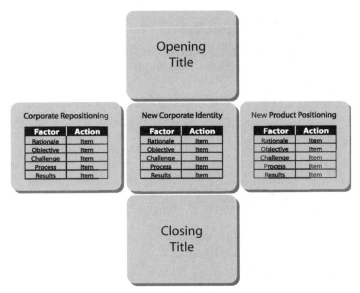

Simple? Yes, especially when you consider that the new team had arrived for their session with me with 48 all-text slides! The revised 5-slide presentation served as a simple and vivid snapshot of their plan to execute their turnaround strategy.

To recap, the five graphic continuity techniques are

1. **Bumper slides**—These are the graphic dividers inserted between major sections of the presentation to serve as clean, quick, and simple transitions.

2. **Indexing/color coding**—This uses a recurring object as an index, high-lighted in different colors to map the different sections of a longer presentation.

3. **Icons**—These express relationships among ideas using recognizable symbolic representations.

4. **Anchor objects**—These create continuity with a recurring image that is an integral part of the illustration.

5. **Anticipation space**—This uses empty areas that are subsequently filled, setting up and then fulfilling subliminal expectations.

The foregoing five simple graphic continuity techniques can have a major impact on the clarity and coherence of your presentations. Artfully used, they can make even a long, complicated story easy for your audience to absorb and remember.

Presenter Focus Revisited

Let me pose a question. Throughout this entire chapter, and in the previous three chapters on graphics, I haven't mentioned Point B or the WIIFY once, while throughout this book, I've repeatedly stressed their importance. Where in the storyboard, or on which slide, do you think you should put your Point B and the audience WIIFY?

The correct answer is nowhere. Point B and the WIIFY don't appear on any slide—they are stated by you, the presenter.

I ask this as a trick question to reinforce the concept of presenter focus. The slides are not the presentation; they are simply presenter support. It is you, the presenter, who must grab your audience at Point A, navigate them through all the parts, and deposit them at Point B.

Imagine a company CEO in a presentation to an audience of potential investors showing the slide in Figure 10.29.

After discussing the various product benefits listed in the slide, the CEO could summarize by saying, "You can see that our product provides a rich set of benefits to our customers," and then move on to the next slide. That action, however, would be an opportunity missed.

Instead, the CEO should add, "This rich set of customer benefits produces repeat business for our company. Repeat business translates into recurring revenues. Recurring revenues translate into shareholder value and an excellent investment opportunity."

That statement contains both the WIIFY and Point B, neither of which appears on the slide. By coming from the presenter, the presenter leads the audience to a conclusion. That conclusion is Aha!

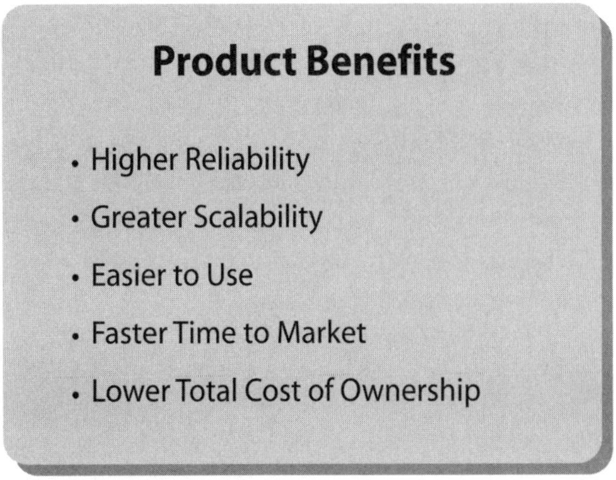

FIGURE 10.29

Where's the WIIFY?

Product Benefits

- Higher Reliability
- Greater Scalability
- Easier to Use
- Faster Time to Market
- Lower Total Cost of Ownership

Graphics and the 35,000-Foot View

Let's recap what you've learned about presentation graphics in the previous four chapters.

The overarching principles that govern all graphics are presenter focus, Less Is More, and minimize eye sweeps. All these principles are particularly important in creating text and numeric slides.

Mix and match text and numeric slides with the other two major graphic options—pictorial and relational slides—to avoid the dreaded Presentation-As-Document Syndrome. Use all these elements to craft the slides that will express your story in a storyboard form.

The storyboard is the 35,000-foot panoramic view of the entire presentation. Microsoft PowerPoint's Slide Sorter View provides this panoramic aspect. The storyboard enables you to check that the graphics convey the sequence clearly. If the transitions from slide to slide or section to section aren't clear, consider reorganizing your slides or crafting strong verbal transitions to make the logic apparent in your narration.

Finally, use the graphic continuity techniques—icons, indexing/color coding, anchor objects, and anticipation space—to help navigate your audience through your presentation. Use bumper slides to help the flow by creating clear transitions between topics.

These tools can ensure that everyone in your audience understands exactly where she is at all times, as well as how any given slide fits into the overall flow of the presentation.

THE ABSOLUTE MINIMUM

- The ultimate technique for checking your flow is to read only the titles of your slides.
- Well-designed graphics not only convey information clearly and attractively, but also help establish the connections among ideas.

PART IV

TELLING YOUR STORY

IN THIS CHAPTER

- The right way to practice presenting
- Techniques to make your delivery seamless
- Solutions to problem phrases

11

IN FRONT OF THE ROOM: BRINGING YOUR STORY TO LIFE

The past few chapters have focused on the visual side of your presentation. Now it's time to take a big step back and think again about your presentation as a whole, particularly about its verbal side.

Verbalization: Shout It Out!

Let's return to the story form, which you first saw in Chapter 6, "Starting Your Story: Capturing Your Audience Immediately" (refer to Figure 6.2). This single form contains the basic building blocks of any presentation story: the opening gambit, point B, the outline, and the Flow Structures.

> 66 Your presentation comes to life only when you add granularity: the specific verbiage you will use to tell your story. 99

The form lays out the overall flow of your presentation story, but because it is at a high level of abstraction (the forest view), it shows only the most salient points. Your presentation comes to life only when you add granularity: the specific verbiage you will use to tell your story.

How do you go from the bare bones presented in the story form to a complete presentation? The answer is through a process of preparation and practice called *verbalization*.

Verbalization means turning your outline into a full-fledged presentation by practicing it beforehand. Speak the actual words you will use in your presentation aloud, accompanied by your slides. Do it just the way you will do it when you are in front of your intended audience. A truly effective presentation is practically impossible without this magic ingredient.

Yet many of my business clients are reluctant to verbalize during our sessions together. Some claim that the presentation isn't "baked" yet—unaware that verbalization moves the baking process along. Others feel self-conscious or uncomfortable about "performing" in front of others. Still others view verbalization as too elementary. Whatever the reason, they try to short-circuit the process, often assuring me, "Oh, don't worry. I'll rehearse my presentation before I have to deliver it, and it'll be just fine."

Unfortunately, I've seen how most businesspeople rehearse their presentations. As the slides flip by on the screen, the presenter glances at each one and says something like, "Okay, with this slide I'm going to say something about our sales revenues...and then with this slide I'll say something about our path to profitability...and then with this next slide I'll show a picture of our lab and talk a little about R&D."

> 66 Speak the actual words you will use in your presentation aloud, accompanied by your slides.... A truly effective presentation is practically impossible without this magic ingredient. 99

Sound familiar? As a form of rehearsal, it is completely unproductive. Talking about your presentation is not an effective method of practicing your presentation—any more than talking about tennis would be a good method of improving your backhand. I call this approach *disembodiment* because it distances you from your presentation.

> 66 Talking about your presentation is not an effective method of practicing your presentation—any more than talking about tennis would be a good method of improving your backhand. 99

A close cousin of disembodiment, and an even more common practice, is mumbling. We've all seen it done. The presenter either clicks through the slides on the computer or flips through the pages of a hard copy of the slides while muttering unintelligible words.

Neither of these methods is verbalization.

The only way to prepare a Power Presentation is to speak it aloud, just as you will on the day of your actual presentation. By talking your way through your entire presentation in advance, by articulating your key points and making the logical connections, by doing a real-time verbalization, you crystallize the ideas in your mind.

Here's a personal perspective: I present nearly every business day of my life, so I don't have to verbalize material I've delivered in one form or another thousands of times before. When I have to present new material, however, I verbalize it extensively in advance. An example is the pyramid presentation I referred to in Chapter 5, "Plotting Your Story: Flow Structures" (refer to Figure 5.1). You'll recall that I often give this presentation at conferences where I describe the essential components of any presentation by starting with the story as the foundation at the base of the pyramid.

Even though I've given variations of this presentation countless times, I still verbalize each new iteration a couple of dozen times in advance. When I have to deliver completely new material, I double that number of repetitions.

Another perspective is my experience with the CEO of a startup technology company. The man, who began his professional career as a scientist, had developed his esoteric technology in his garage and then bootstrapped his company without ever having to make presentations. But when his technology took off and his company was about to go public, he knew that he would have to stand and deliver the IPO roadshow. He retained my services and we went through all the steps you've learned in this book, except for the verbalization.

> 66 The only way to prepare a Power Presentation is to speak it aloud, just as you will on the day of your actual presentation. 99

On the morning of the day he was to deliver his roadshow to the investment banking team that would be selling his offering, he panicked. I printed his slides on paper, spread them out on a conference room table, and asked him to talk through them. But he stammered as he did, and his panic intensified. I asked him to start again. As he worked his way through the slides the second time, he stammered less and less. I asked him to do it again and again.

> 66 Each time you verbalize your presentation, and each time you deliver it before a live audience, you should expect the words of your narrative to vary slightly. 99

By the fifth run-through, his stammering had disappeared; by the sixth, he was beginning to develop continuity; by lunchtime, when the bankers arrived, he was able to deliver a positively fluid presentation. The solid foundation of the well-developed story and graphics combined with verbalization gave the apprehensive presenter the comfort level he needed.

When you verbalize, speak from your storyboard form (refer to Figure 10.1 in Chapter 10, "Using Graphics to Help Your Story Flow"). See and use this panoramic view to navigate through your presentation. Before long, you'll find that your Less Is More slides act as your guide. Each bullet, written on a single line, serves as a headline and triggers the body text from you. Remember how the Roman orator used the columns in the Forum as his prompts. The same happens when you use your slides as your Roman columns.

Each time you verbalize your presentation, and each time you deliver it before a live audience, you should expect the words of your narrative to vary slightly. The logic of your well-honed outline and your improved comfort level will guarantee that every time you deliver your presentation, you'll express your key ideas clearly and persuasively. That's the magic of verbalization.

Spaced Learning

Educators distinguish between distributed learning and massed learning. *Distributed learning*, occurring over time, is the more efficient method because it allows for absorption and understanding. Distributed learning is a synonym for spaced learning; *massed learning* is a synonym for cramming.

Every schoolboy and schoolgirl in America has heard the story about how Abraham Lincoln wrote the Gettysburg Address on the back of an envelope. The implication is that he dashed off the classic speech with little or no advance preparation.

There are several variations of this tale. In his Pulitzer Prize-winning book, *Lincoln at Gettysburg*, Garry Wills describes several other lesser-known versions of the same story that have Lincoln "considering [the speech] on the way to a photographer's

shop in Washington, writing it on a piece of card-
board...as the train took him on the 80-mile
trip...penciling it...on the night before the dedica-
tion, writing it...on the morning of the day he had
to deliver it, or even composing it in his head as
Everett [the prior speaker at the Gettysburg cere-
mony] spoke."

> 66 Whenever I ask my clients
> if they ever whip their own
> presentations together at the
> last minute, I usually get a
> round of sheepish grins. 99

Maybe the appeal of these stories comes from the
fact that so many businesspeople prepare their own presentations in this fashion.
Charles M. Boesenberg, now the CEO of NetIQ, was the president of MIPS, a semiconductor design company, and a participant in the roadshow for its public offering
in 1989. When Chuck later became the CEO of Central Point Software, he retained
my services for his IPO roadshow. I introduced Chuck to the same story techniques
you've been learning here: the framework form, brainstorming, clustering, and Flow
Structures.

Halfway through the first day of the program, Chuck broke into a big grin and said,
"At MIPS, we did all of this in the taxi on the way to the airport to begin our roadshow!"

Chuck is not alone. Whenever I ask my clients if they ever whip their own presentations together at the last minute, I usually get a round of sheepish grins. Their variations on the theme include

- "Oh, I didn't have time to do my presentation, but I'll wing it!"
- "I'm running late in a meeting, can you deliver my pitch for me?"
- "I won't have time to work on this, so have Marketing put something together."

Finally, there's the approach that, unfortunately, far too many businesspeople use:
"Let's see, I can use three of Tom's slides, six of Dick's, and four of Harry's." I've
named this method *Frankenstein-body-parts*.

If any of those approaches sounds familiar, it might make you feel better to believe
that Abraham Lincoln produced his masterful Gettysburg Address in much the same
way. However, just the opposite is true. Garry Wills gives the lie to what he calls that
"silly but persistent myth" by detailing the complex history of Lincoln's creation of
the Gettysburg Address. Wills describes how it arose out of a background of popular
nineteenth-century interest in classical rhetoric, Lincoln's own immersion in literature and the Bible, a lifetime of study and practice, and his admiration for the oratory of Daniel Webster. Wills adds about Lincoln, "He was a slow writer, who liked to
sort out his points and tighten his logic and phrasing. This is the process vouched for
in every other case of Lincoln's memorable public statements."

Just for good measure, Wills also tells us that Lincoln combined verbalization with spaced learning: "This surely is the secret of Lincoln's eloquence: he not only read aloud, to think his way into sounds, but wrote as a way of ordering his thoughts."

Wills then puts the improvisation myth about the Gettysburg speech completely to rest. He cites several specific pieces of historic evidence indicating that Lincoln organized his information and ideas in Washington at least two days before the speech and continued to work on the text at multiple points along the way to the Gettysburg site. Then, on that memorable day of November 19, 1863, Lincoln rose "with a sheet or two" to deliver it. All this for a speech that was just 272 words long!

> " Presenters who recognize the value of spaced learning report that when they revisit their presentation or speech after a brief interval away from it, they can quickly see half a dozen ways to improve it. "

From the sublime oratory of Abraham Lincoln to the mundane hobby of puzzles, veteran crossword fans know that when they become stuck with a puzzle, they put it aside briefly. When they return to it a while later, they are unstuck. Presenters who recognize the value of spaced learning report that when they revisit their presentation or speech after a brief interval away from it, they can quickly see half a dozen ways to improve it. This is the result of seeing the presentation from a new viewpoint, or perhaps the result of letting the unconscious mind process the material while the conscious mind is otherwise engaged. Moreover, the result of this fresh perspective creates a greater command of the presentation and makes the presenter feel, as well as appear, more confident.

With all these advantages to spaced learning, why do so many presenters relegate preparing their presentations to the last minute? Most businesspeople, like you, are constantly overloaded, pressured, and rushed. However, if you accept the view that every presentation is a mission-critical event, those excuses are invalid.

We're all familiar with Andy Warhol's comment that everybody will be famous for 15 minutes. I'd extend Warhol's observation to say that every presenter has 15 or 30 or 60 minutes—whatever time is allotted or assigned—to get the audience to Aha! Wouldn't you want every single one of those minutes to be all that it can be? Wouldn't you want to employ every tool and technique at your disposal to grab your audience's minds at the beginning, navigate them through all the parts, never letting go, until you deposit them at Point B?

By the way, I practice what I preach. Most of the material in this book has evolved over the course of 15 years since I started Power Presentations, except for the section you've just read. I decided to write it after I read the Wills book. It took me 37 drafts written over three days, not counting the additional drafts I did with input from my editorial consultant and publisher.

If you've benefited from reading this section, you can thank spaced learning. You can also use the same tool to your own advantage.

Internal Linkages

You'll be building your presentations using the key elements contained in the story form. Consider these elements as building blocks that need mortar to hold them together. The glue is a set of narrative tools called *linkages*: meaningful verbal transitions from one slide to the next and from one part of the presentation to the next.

The importance of linkages is best illustrated by returning to the investment banking conferences I first described in Chapter 5. I attend these conferences because they let me observe many presentations in a short time. At each conference, I get to see dozens of executives, each of them experienced, poised, and confident speakers, make their management presentations. Yet I see the lion's share of them proceed through each presentation in the same manner: The presenter clicks to a slide on the screen and says, "Now I'd like to talk about…" and then she talks about that slide. Then the presenter clicks to the next slide and says, "Now I'd like to talk about…" and she talks about that slide. A click to the next slide, and the presenter says, "Now I'd like to talk about…" and so on, throughout the presentation.

This trite phrase is not only a boring cliché, but it also destroys any continuity or flow. In effect, it means each slide starts the presentation anew. I call this *rebooting*, and it presents a major problem for the audience. With no context for the diverse ideas and no connection among the ideas, the audience is stranded at the level of the trees, seeing only one tree at a time, with no idea of how one tree relates to another. The missing connections are the verbal glue that the presenter must provide.

These connections take two main forms: *internal linkages*, which are statements that tie together the various parts of your presentation, and *external linkages*, which are statements that tie the various parts of your presentation to your audience. We cover the internal linkages, of which there are 12, in this chapter and save the external linkages for the next one.

Twelve Internal Linkages

Use these internal linkages liberally throughout your presentation, and make it easy for your audience to follow your flow:

> 66 The missing connections are the verbal glue that the presenter must provide. 99

1. **Reference the Flow Structure**—Make repeated references to your primary Flow Structure as you track through your presentation.

2. **Logical transition**—Close your outbound subject; lead in to your inbound subject.

3. **Cross-Reference**—Make forward and backward references to other subjects in your presentation.

4. **Rhetorical question**—Pose a relevant question, and then provide the answer.

5. **Recurring theme**—Establish an example or data point early in your presentation, and then make several references to it throughout your presentation.

6. **Symmetry**—Establish an example or data point early in your presentation, and never mention it again until the end.

7. **Mantra**—Use a catch phrase or slogan repeatedly.

8. **Internal summary**—Pause at major transitions and recapitulate.

9. **Enumeration**—Present related concepts as a suite and count down through each of them.

10. **Do the math**—Put numeric information in perspective.

11. **Point B reinforcement**—Restate your call to action at several points throughout your presentation.

12. **Say your company name**—State your company, product, or service name often.

Let's look more closely at each of the 12 internal linkages, with brief examples of each.

Reference the Flow Structure

Although all the other internal linkages are options that you can mix and match and use as needed, the first—referencing the Flow Structure—is not an option, but a necessity. It provides yet another way for you to bring your audience up from the level of the trees and give them a continuing view of the forest.

Here's how it works: If you've chosen Problem/Solution as the Flow Structure for your

> 66 Although all the other internal linkages are options you can mix and match and use as needed, the first—referencing the Flow Structure—is not an option, but a necessity. 99

presentation, keep referring to the problem your business is addressing. Throughout your presentation, use sentences such as, "So, you can see how our unique solution addresses the problem that affects millions of people."

Similarly, if you've chosen the Opportunity/Leverage Flow Structure, keep referring to the large opportunity your company's products or services are deploying to leverage that opportunity.

Or, if you've chosen a Numerical Flow Structure, such as "10 Reasons to Buy from Us," track the countdown (or count up, if you follow David Letterman) for the audience. Let them know where you are at pivotal points in your presentation: "Here's the first reason…. Now reason number two…. Finally, here's the tenth and best reason of all…."

Logical Transition

The logical transition is the simplest and most straightforward type of internal linkage. It simply means clearly stating the logical connection between one idea and the next.

For example, suppose you are one of a team of presenters offering a detailed account of your company's business and future plans. If you completed your portion of the presentation by saying, "Well, that about wraps up what I have to say. Now I'd like my colleague Nancy to come up and say what she has to say," you wouldn't be making a connection between your material and Nancy's. There would be no logical transition. It would be like a relay racer dropping the baton on the track, forcing the next runner on the team to bend over to pick it up. With this awkward transition, you would let your audience slip from your navigational grasp and allow them to drift. If instead you said, "Now that you've seen the business opportunity and how we're going after it, I'm sure you'd like to know how we're positioned financially to pursue that opportunity. Our CFO Nancy will now come up and tell you." That would be a clear linkage. You would be providing closure of the outbound (your part of the presentation) and a natural lead in to the inbound (Nancy's part of the presentation). You would be passing the baton directly and retaining your grip on the audience's attention.

Think of the logical transition as verbal kin to the visual bumper slide discussed in Chapter 9, "Making the Numbers Sing." Both transitions provide the closure/lead function, clearing your audience's minds between sections of your presentation in the same way that sorbet cleanses a diner's palate between courses of a fine meal.

Cross-Reference

The cross-reference is another effective form of linkage. Say you introduce a technical concept early in the presentation, but you don't want to drill down with a detailed explanation at that point. Simply make a forward reference by saying you'll cover the concept in greater detail later. Moreover, when you get to that concept, make a backward reference by saying, "Now let's turn to the subject I introduced earlier."

> 66 If you do make a forward reference, remember to complete the circuit by delivering the discussion point you promised. 99

Forward and backward references are very powerful tools, if you use them properly. The forward reference, however, can backfire. How many times have you heard a presenter make a forward reference and then fail to deliver? If the audience remembers the reference and realizes it never materialized, they feel disappointed. Even if they don't consciously remember, they will most likely have a vague feeling that "something was left out." Both alternatives alienate the audience. If you do make a forward reference, remember to complete the circuit by delivering the discussion point you promised.

By contrast, the backward reference is an almost fail-safe tool. When you link back to an idea you presented earlier in your presentation, you get to reinforce that idea. It also indicates that your material is well organized and coherent. The subliminal message: effective management.

When you are part of a team presentation, you can also cross-reference people. Say one another's names a couple of times during the presentation, preferably first names: "As Frank explained, our R&D division has several of the world's top experts in the field." Such statements send the message that you work well together.

Rhetorical Question

For a short, pivotal transition, you can use the rhetorical question. Pose a question that grows out of your outbound point or one that leads logically to your inbound point, and then provide the answer.

For example, after describing what your company has done over the past year, you can transition to your future plans with the rhetorical question, "Where do we go from here?" After explaining how your company intends to take advantage of a major new market opportunity, you can transition to your operating plan by asking, "How are we going to implement that?" Alternatively, you can transition from your company's business results to a comparison with other companies in the field by asking, "How do we stack up against the competition?" In each case, go on to provide the answer.

Limit your use of the rhetorical question; too many of them can sound contrived. The wording can also sound contrived. The question, "Have we set up customer call centers staffed by college-educated personnel to handle complex service issues?," rings artificial. Couch your questions in terms your audience might use, such as, "How do we handle complex service issues?"

> 66 Limit your use of the rhetorical question; too many of them can sound contrived. 99

Recurring Theme

A *recurring theme* is a subject that weaves its way throughout your presentation. Say you used a customer anecdote about a woman named Louise King as your opening gambit. You can then reference Louise King, and the millions of satisfied customers like her, several times throughout your presentation. When you describe the efficiency of your manufacturing processes, you can say, "Because of the low unit cost of our product, we're able to sell it at a price that people like Louise King can afford." Or, when you explain the marketing campaign that successfully launched your product, you can say, "Louise King saw one of our full-page ads in *USA Today* and called the 800 number listed there."

Symmetry

An alternative use of the recurring theme option is to reference the theme at the beginning of your presentation and then never mention it again until the end. This form of linkage is called *symmetry*. You could cite customer Louise King in your opening gambit and then at the very end say, "Remember Louise King?" The resulting bookend effect provides resolution and therefore subliminal satisfaction to your audience.

Mantra

A *mantra* is a running phrase or slogan you repeat several times during your presentation. This technique goes all the way back to the Greek orators, who called it *anaphora*.

Many modern-day orators have used the mantra to great effect. Winston Churchill rallied the beleaguered British people during World War II with a stirring speech in which he repeated the phrase "we shall" a total of 12 times: "...we shall go on to the end, we shall fight in France, we shall fight on the seas and oceans, we shall fight with growing confidence and growing strength in the air, we shall defend our Island, whatever the cost may be...."

Martin Luther King, Jr., used the phrase "I have a dream" 16 times in his historic civil rights speech.

John F. Kennedy's memorable inaugural address is famous for his use of the word "ask" five times in three sentences: "And so, my fellow Americans: Ask not what your country can do for you, ask what you can do for your country. My fellow citizens of the world: Ask not what America will do for you, but what together we can do for the freedom of man. Finally, whether you are citizens of America or citizens of the world, ask of us here the same high standards of strength and sacrifice which we ask of you."

> 66 The mantra could just turn out to be the best-remembered phrase or sentence from your presentation, so choose it carefully. If you develop a mantra, make it pithy, concise, and appealing. 99

What is not as famous is that, within that same 14-minute speech, Kennedy used the word "let" 16 times.

Corporations spend enormous amounts of time and money on specialized marketing consultants to develop corporate slogans or tag lines. Think of Microsoft's "Where do you want to go today?" or Cisco's "Are you ready?" or Intel's "Intel Inside."

Your mantra needn't be just your company's slogan. You can create one that is specific to your presentation. If you were presenting your company's turnaround strategy and the changes your company has made, you could say repeatedly, "That was then, this is now."

The mantra could just turn out to be the best-remembered phrase or sentence from your presentation, so choose it carefully. If you develop a mantra, make it pithy, concise, and appealing. Most important, be sure that your mantra supports your key persuasive theme: your Point B.

Internal Summary

The internal summary is a way of clearing your audience's minds and cleansing their palates by pausing at a pivotal point or two in your presentation and saying, "Let's review what we've covered so far."

Your headlong forward progress is quite well known to you but is brand-new to your audience. They need a moment to digest what you've said and shown. When they don't get that moment, the result can be the MEGO syndrome or, worse, an interruption that throws your presentation off onto a tangent.

No matter how intelligent your audience, they cannot take in your ideas at the rate at which they are output. In football, the wide receivers know exactly where they are going and the defensive backs do not, giving the receivers a distinct advantage. In football, however, each team gets a chance to switch roles. In presentations, the presenter and audience roles remain fixed, so it is essential that you give your audience the advantage by letting them know exactly where you are going at all times.

> 66 In presentations…it is essential that you give your audience the advantage by letting them know exactly where you are going at all times. 99

After you've finished your brief internal summary, you can resume your forward progress by leading into the next section of your presentation. Think of this linkage technique as a miniature application of the "tell 'em what you're gonna tell 'em" concept.

Enumeration

Say you have four new products in your product line to present. Rather than stepping through the four one at a time, tell your audience that there are four in all. Give them the forest view, rather than one tree at a time.

Introduce them as a suite: "We're announcing today a new line of four products, each targeted to a different market segment." Then discuss each one in detail as necessary: "Product A is ideal for the beginner because it offers…." After discussing all four, briefly recap the whole product line: "As you can see, these four products can serve virtually anyone who needs…."

Use enumeration sparingly, however. Don't give your audience six sub-themes under each main topic and eight sub-heads under each of the six sub-themes. Your audience can't follow your left-brain thinking that far down. They can't keep track of that many levels of detail, nor should you expect them to. When you enumerate, stay with one list and count your way through it concisely.

Do the Math

When you discuss numeric information in your presentation, provide your audience with perspective by comparing, contrasting, or interpreting the numbers for them.

For instance, "The debate ran 45 minutes, which means that each candidate had about 22 minutes. In tallying the total debate, and tracking the calls to action, one candidate stated his Point B 21 times and the other 27 times, an average of one Point B per minute." Or, "Dangerous drug interactions are a serious problem. Less than one-tenth of 1% of medication prescriptions produce drug interactions serious enough to require hospitalization, but that

> 66 Use enumeration sparingly, however. Don't give your audience six sub-themes under each main topic and eight sub-heads under each of the six sub-themes. 99

number is 2.7 million annually. Less than 2% of these interactions are fatal, but that number is 50,000 people, which is more than all the people killed in auto accidents each year."

Point B Reinforcement

As the story form indicates, it's important to reinforce your Point B at the beginning and end of your presentation. Experience shows that the two parts of any presentation audiences remember best are the beginning and the end. Therefore, be sure to highlight your Point B, your call to action, in those key places.

However, in any other than the briefest presentation, you can reinforce your Point B several times. It's the best way to ensure that your audience grasps Point B, remembers it, and understands how each of your persuasive points supports it.

Say Your Company Name

When making a business presentation, it's almost unavoidable to refer to your company, so mentioning it is a natural form of linkage. However, be sure to make that reference by name: "Acme Widgets," rather than "our company," or "the company," or "we." This reinforces your company's name in your audience's minds—an important consideration because so many presentations occur in competitive circumstances, such as conferences, where you are fighting for mindshare against many other companies.

It is also basic brand identity. Businesses today spend a great deal of time, effort, and money to develop their corporate images in logos, colors, and slogans; they spend even more time, effort, and money disseminating that image on everything from coffee mugs to shirts to baseball caps. It is much more time- and cost-efficient to have the company spokesperson promote the brand live and in person.

Internal Linkages in Action

How many linkages should you use in your presentation? The best answer is, "Enough." Use as many linkages as you need to create a presentation that is a tightly unified whole. The end result will be a presentation in which each element relates to the next and all the elements lead to a single conclusion: Point B.

Pick and choose from among the internal linkage options that feel appropriate for your presentation and your speaking style. Plan the linkages as you

> 66 Use as many linkages as you need to create a presentation that is a tightly unified whole. 99

develop your presentation, practice them every time you verbalize, and then deliver them when you present.

Phraseology

The ultimate phase of bringing your presentation to life is selecting the words you'll use to tell your story, or what I call *phraseology*.

You'll remember from Chapter 5 that the Flow Structure I use in my Power Presentations program and in this book is Problem/Solution—that is, in each of the essential aspects of a presentation, I show you how not to do it and then how to do it correctly. To maintain that consistency in addressing verbiage, I've collected a handful of the most commonly used phrases in presentations (I'm sure you'll recognize them, too), each of which creates a problem for the presenter. I then provide you with the correct way to state the same idea. The first example is perhaps the most common of all:

    ▽ "Now I'd like to...."

Sound familiar? You've probably heard this phrase almost as often as I have. It's virtually boilerplate not only in business presentations, but also in political speeches, college lectures, church sermons, award acceptances, wedding toasts—the list is endless.

What's wrong with this phrase? It's presenter-focused. It implies that the presenter is making an exclusive decision without any regard for the audience: "I don't care what you'd like to do; this is what I'd like to do."

It's also vague and indefinite. If you'd like to do it, why not just go ahead and do it? How many times have you been on an airplane and, upon landing, heard the flight attendant say, "I'd like to be the first to welcome you to San Francisco." How about simply, "Welcome to San Francisco"?

The fix: Make the phrase audience-focused, inclusive, and very definite. Drop the word *like* and simply say:

    ▲ "I'm going to talk about...."

Or become even more inclusive by inviting the audience to join you: Shift to the first-person plural using one of these options:

    ▲ "Let's look at...."

    ▲ "Let's...."

What does the following phrase imply?

▽ "Like I said...."

This phrase is a form of backward reference, an attempt to link to a point earlier in the presentation. Unfortunately, the specific language suggests that your audience didn't understand your pearls of wisdom the first time you said them, so you are now going to repeat yourself to bring them up to your speed, all of which is condescending to your audience.

The phrase is also poor English. *Like* is the wrong word; it should be *As*.

Now this doesn't mean you should avoid backward references. Use them extensively (have you noticed how often I've used them in this book?). Backward references are powerful tools for continuity and reinforcement.

If you do use them, however, do so with the proper connecting word: "As I said," not "Like I said." But that still leaves the phrase presenter-focused. Better to give your audience credit for having understood and remembered what you said by using one of the following options:

▲ "As you recall...."

▲ "We discussed earlier...."

▲ "We saw...."

▲ "Remember...."

What's the problem with the following phrase?

▽ "I'll tell you very quickly...."

This phrase implies that you're apologizing for your own material, that what you have to say isn't very important, so you will hurry through it. By apologizing, you're saying you didn't care enough about your audience to have prepared your presentation carefully.

There are many variations of the apology, as the following phrases demonstrate:

▽ "I'm running out of time...."

▽ "If you could read this slide...."

▽ "This is a busy slide...."

▽ "This isn't my slide...."

▽ "Disregard this...."

▽ "Before I begin...."

I'll bet you've heard every one of these at least once in your career.

Never apologize, and *always* prepare properly. By apologizing, you're just drawing your audience's attention to the deficiencies in your presentation. Omit any topic that does not deserve your audience's time and attention. Present with pride any topic that is important enough to include in your presentation.

> 66 *Never* apologize, and *always* prepare properly. 99

What's wrong with this next phrase?

▽ "Acme listens to its customer and meets his requirements...."

The problem with this phrase is that it's gender-specific. Are all your customers males? Probably not, unless your company makes a product such as after-shave lotion. The issue here isn't political correctness, but rather accuracy. Make your statement universal by going plural:

▲ "Acme listens to its customers and meets their requirements...."

In the English language, the plural pronoun *their* has no gender marking, so you can use it to refer to men, women, or both.

Here are three other problematic phrases:

▽ "We believe...."

▽ "We think...."

▽ "We feel...."

Each of these phrases introduces an element of uncertainty. You believe something to be true, but is it really? You introduce doubt, even if only subliminally, in the minds of your audience. Your job instead is to convey certainty. The way to get from doubt to certainty is to switch from the conditional to the declarative mood. Recast the entire sentence to eliminate the offending phrase.

Rather than saying:

▽ "With this large opportunity and our superior technology, I think you'll see that Acme is positioned for growth."

Say:

▲ "With this large opportunity and our superior technology, you'll see that Acme is positioned for growth."

> 66 The way to get from doubt to certainty is to switch from the conditional to the declarative mood. 99

The simple removal of the "I think" phrase strengthens the impact of the entire sentence.

This is not to say that, when the outcome is uncertain, you should make forward-looking statements or forecasts. That's risky business. In such cases, use the conditional mood, but instead of using the weak words *think*, *believe*, and *feel*, shift to any of these much stronger options:

▲ "We're confident...."

▲ "We're convinced...."

▲ "We're optimistic...."

▲ "We expect...."

What's wrong with the following sentence?

▽ "Acme does not view the competition as significant."

There are several problems here. For one thing, the statement is arrogant. It suggests that Acme's management isn't taking the issue of competition seriously. For another, it's stupid. Any competition is significant.

On a purely verbal level, however, the sentence is also negative because of the dreaded *not* word. Most human beings, businesspeople in particular, react negatively to negativity. Recast the sentence to remove the arrogance, the stupidity, and the dreaded *not* word:

▲ "Acme has strong competitive advantages."

Here's another form of negativity:

▽ "What we're not is...."

Far too many presentations begin with a description of the company's business by telling what they are not; instead, they should tell what they are.

For the final problematic phrase, let's flash back to January 1987. President Ronald Reagan had not expressed his position on a very sensitive subject roiling in the media: the involvement of his administration in the Iran-Contra scandal. Reagan finally agreed to tell all in a press conference. The headlines in the next day's newspapers carried his key statement:

▽ "Mistakes were made."

But Reagan didn't say who made the mistakes.

Now, let's flash forward 10 years. In January 1997, President Bill Clinton had not expressed his position on a very sensitive subject roiling in the media: the involvement of his administration in improper, possibly illegal, fundraising activities. Clinton finally agreed to tell all in a press conference. The headlines in the next day's newspapers carried his key statement:

▽ "Mistakes were made."

History repeats itself. Both Reagan and Clinton couched their statements using the passive voice. This grammatical construction tells what was done, but it doesn't say who did it. The result is that the speaker sounds as if he is trying to avoid responsibility through fudging and obfuscation.

> 66 Passive voice sentences remove the doer of the action and, with it, remove management—and the presenter—from any responsibility or culpability for the action, whether bad or good. 99

This is accepted practice in politics, where Reagan and Clinton (and generations of politicians before and after them) were striving to protect their associates, their constituencies, and themselves. This is not at all acceptable in business, where accountability is paramount. Passive voice sentences remove the doer of the action and, with it, remove management—and the presenter—from any responsibility or culpability for the action, whether bad or good.

All the previous examples are not meant to be merely a lesson in syntax, but a lesson in persuasive psychology. The difference between the passive voice and the active voice is subtle in grammar but profound in impact. Avoid the former; use the latter. Put the doer back into the sentence; put management back into the equation.

Instead of saying

▽ "Mistakes were made."

▽ "Progress is being made."

▽ "The error rate is being reduced."

Say:

▲ "We made a mistake."

▲ "We're making progress."

▲ "We have reduced our error rate."

When you put the doer back into the action, you put management back into the equation. The subliminal takeaway is effective management.

Practice Really Does Make Perfect (or At Least Gets You a Whole Lot Closer)

After you've developed your lucid story and expressive graphics, verbalize your presentation in advance. Do multiple verbalizations spaced out over time. As you do, think about and practice the specific language you'll use to convey your ideas. Select and plan clear internal linkages. Monitor your phraseology to develop a positive, respectful, and confident vocabulary.

Just as particular styles of slide design can hinder or enhance your presentations, particular words, phrases, and sentences can offend your audience or help win them over. By studying your verbal options in advance and diligently practicing your best choices, you can make your words sing, help your story flow, and bring your presentation to life.

THE ABSOLUTE MINIMUM

- The only way to prepare a Power Presentation is to speak it aloud, just as you will on the day of your actual presentation.

- Use as many linkages as you need to create a presentation that is a tightly unified whole.

12

CUSTOMIZING YOUR PRESENTATION

A Face in the Crowd

On my very first day as an undergraduate at New York University, I attended the orientation session for incoming freshmen in a state of suspended animation. I had left behind the camaraderie and cinder-block walls of a New York City public high school, and now, alone and apart from my close friends of four years, I entered the marble halls of NYU's Gould Memorial Chapel. I was a solitary speck in a sea of strangers, all of us intimidated by our imposing surroundings and further humbled by our requisite freshmen headdress: bright violet beanies.

My awe was heightened when I saw an array of austere deans and professors in their black gowns, seated on the stage, looking down at us lowly frosh. As each of these august sages stood in turn to address us, their stentorian tones and crisp articulation echoing off the domed ceiling of the chapel, I recalled how differently my high school teachers had spoken, with the strident twang and staccato pace of a hardcore New York accent. I was still in the same city, but I might as well have been at Oxford or Cambridge.

The most impressive and most articulate dean of the group rose to speak. "Gentlemen," he began (for there were no women at NYU at that time), "by now you realize that your life here at the university is going to be vastly different from high school. However, there is one high school practice that we have carried forward. We take attendance."

At that, he reached under his gown, into his coat pocket, and pulled out a set of what looked like business cards. "These are your attendance records," he said. Then, as if holding up a bridge hand, he fanned out the cards in one hand and, with his other, reached forward and plucked one of the cards. Reading from it, he said, "Suppose you're Jerry Weissman…."

Imagine my reaction. I couldn't have been more stunned if I'd heard the voice of God reverberating my name from the dome.

I wasn't the only one to react. Several other freshmen sitting nearby, whom I'd just met, turned to look at me, and their stirring rippled through the audience like a wave.

I later learned that the dean's selection of my card was completely accidental and arbitrary, but that he always picked an actual card from among the members of each new audience. I also learned that he happened to be the chairman of the Speech Department.

In time, Professor Ormond J. Drake became my mentor. Later still, he became my supervisor when I served as an instructor in his department, my sponsor when he gave me a consulting assignment at a Wall Street brokerage house, and my colleague when I produced and directed an episode of his talk-show series for CBS Television. But to this day, what I remember most about Professor Drake is the startling Aha!, which I experienced when he spoke my name in the middle of the welcoming speech he'd given to generations of entering freshmen.

That's the power of customization.

The Illusion of the First Time

Many business presentations contain information that must be conveyed repeatedly, to multiple audiences. For example, a salesperson might have to present a new product to many different groups of customers, or a human resources manager might have to explain the new company benefits plan to dozens of small groups of employees. In the IPO roadshow world, company officers must make their presentations to many, many groups of investors. Typically, they give 60–80 pitches over a period from two to three weeks, often 6–8 pitches on any given day.

> 66 The challenge for the presenter is to find ways to...achieve "the illusion of the first time." 99

Under these circumstances, keeping your presentation fresh and vital is difficult. In part, this is a matter of energy and focus. When you have to make the same points for the third, tenth, or fiftieth time, it's hard to feel the same sense of enthusiasm, spontaneity, and excitement as the first time. It's all too easy to become bored with your presentation and let your attention flag. When you go into autopilot, however, your presentation comes across as "mailed in," and the result is an audience that is uninvolved, unmoved, and unconvinced.

The challenge for the presenter is to find ways to overcome this downside, to achieve "the illusion of the first time." I've borrowed this phrase from the jargon of stage actors, who often have to perform the same role in the same play hundreds of times (if they're fortunate enough to have a role in a hit production), while conveying to each new audience the sense that every speech and every action is completely spontaneous.

Contrast the theatrical approach to that of the world of journalism. In journalism, an article that can run any time in any edition of a publication is called an *evergreen*. This relegates the content of the article to mere filler. Never, ever make your presentation an evergreen. As Shakespeare had Hamlet say, "Suit the action to the word, the word to the action." Create the illusion of the first time, every time.

The key to creating that illusion is to make a deliberate effort to focus your energy every time you present. If the thought of repeating the same material over and over again makes your spirit wane, remember the example of baseball immortal Joe DiMaggio. A reporter once said to the Yankee Clipper, "Joe, you always seem to play ball with the same intensity. You run out every grounder and race after every fly ball, even in the dog days of August when the Yankees have a big lead in the pennant race and there's nothing on the line. How do you do it?"

> 66 The key to creating that illusion is to make a deliberate effort to focus your energy every time you present. 99

DiMaggio replied, "I always remind myself that there might be someone in the stands who never saw me play before."

In the same way, treat each and every iteration of every presentation as if no one in your audience has ever seen you present before. The equivalent of running out every grounder and racing after every fly ball is to generate your enthusiasm and pump up your energy every time.

> 66 ...treat each and every iteration of every presentation as if no one in your audience has ever seen you present before. 99

However, energy alone is not enough. With all the will in the world, it's difficult to create the illusion of the first time unless you modify your presentation for each new audience. Fortunately, as a business presenter, you enjoy a freedom that stage actors don't have: You can reshape your script and give every performance a new dose of freshness and spontaneity. Does this mean you have to change your recurring presentation each time? Not at all. You can customize the core material using the following techniques. You can use these very same techniques to customize a one-time-only presentation, as well as every presentation you ever give to every audience.

External Linkages

The internal linkages in the previous chapter bind together the components of your presentation, but it's equally important to bond your presentation (and you, as the presenter) to each specific audience. You can achieve that with external linkages: words, phrases, stories, and other materials you insert throughout your presentation to make it fresh. The seven external linkages are

1. **Direct reference**—Mention specifically, by name, one or more members of your audience.

2. **Mutual reference**—Make reference to a person, a company, or an organization related to both you and your audience.

3. **Ask questions**—Address a question directly to one or more members of your audience.

4. **Contemporize**—Make reference to what is happening today.

5. **Localize**—Make reference to the venue of your presentation.

6. **Data**—Make reference to current information that links to and supports your message.

> 66 You can reshape your script and give every performance a new dose of freshness and spontaneity. 99

7. **Customized the opening graphic**—Start your presentation with a slide that includes your audience, the location, and the date.

> 66 Be careful to make all direct references positive and non-controversial. 99

Let's consider each external linkage, along with illustrative examples.

Direct Reference

A direct reference is a specific mention, by name, of one or more members of your audience. This is the technique Professor Ormond Drake used during my orientation at NYU, and you can measure its effectiveness by the fact that I still recall the moment, decades later.

There are several ways to incorporate direct references. One is to refer to audience members to illustrate your key points: "Our services can help reduce the amount of time you spend traveling on business. Take Steve, here, as an example. Steve told me that he's been on the road 12 days this month. With our services, Steve can...."

Another way is to tell a story related to the audience or to specific audience members: "As some of you might know, I've worked with your firm before. Last year, Sharon and I developed a joint plan for launching a new program...."

"During the break, I was speaking with Howard, and he told me that your company is about to move to new headquarters. You'll be interested to know that our product can help streamline the process...."

Be careful to make all direct references positive and non-controversial. Only quote statements or tell stories that reveal the audience member in a positive light. And, of course, never violate a confidence.

Mutual Reference

A *mutual reference* is a reference to a person, a company, or an organization that is in some way linked to both you and your audience. Think of a mutual reference as a tasteful, appropriate form of name-dropping. For example, in pitching your services to Company A, you might want to describe the work you did for Company B, which has a close business alliance with Company A, or the work you did for Company C, whose CEO sits on the board of Company A, or the work you did for Company D, which is Company A's largest and most-respected industry rival.

> 66 Before using a mutual reference, however, check into the politics of the three-way relationship. 99

Before using a mutual reference, however, check into the politics of the three-way relationship. Avoid stumbling into a personal or business feud you didn't know existed. Be certain that your audience will view every connection as an affirmation.

Ask Questions

Although a question is effective as an opening gambit, you can also use the same technique at any point in almost any presentation. By addressing a question directly to one or more members of your audience, you create an effective external linkage.

There are several ways to use questions. One is the Scott Cook approach of polling the audience. This is a quick way of gauging their interest in or receptivity to a particular concept in your presentation: "How many of your companies plan to increase spending on information technology during the next year? May I have a show of hands? Quite a few, I see. Our new software system can help you get the most out of any new technology you do purchase. Here's how it works...."

If you do use this technique, however, be prepared for all contingencies: all of the above, some of the above, and none of the above. Be prepared with a follow-up to each contingency.

Another question technique is to invite audience members to share ideas, reactions, or stories, which you can use as a springboard for further discussion: "Think back to the last time you had a negative experience with airplane travel. What was the problem? Any volunteers? Okay, Reggie, tell us about it...."

Yet another technique is to use questions to point the audience toward a predetermined conclusion: "What sort of features would your company need in a new communications system? Where on the list would you rank reliability? Why is that? What happens when your system is down? To address that concern, let's look at some independent data on the reliability of our latest system...."

Asking questions is an excellent way of engaging your audience. Getting people to think about issues and discuss them aloud turns your presentation from a one-way transmission into a two-way interaction, increasing your audience's interest and involvement.

However, questions do inject a note of unpredictability. An audience member's response to one of your questions can raise an irrelevant issue or jump ahead to an idea you will cover later in the presentation. Avoid such detours by politely defining the parameters of your topic.

Preplan the questions you will use, and phrase them carefully. Don't make them heavy-handed

> 66 Getting people to think about issues and discuss them aloud turns your presentation from a one-way transmission into a two-way interaction, increasing your audience's interest and involvement. 99

and obvious. Based on your knowledge of the audience, word the questions to maximize your chance of eliciting the kinds of answers you want.

> 66 Preplan the questions you will use, and phrase them carefully. 99

Contemporize

This technique involves making a reference to the most current of events, what is happening today. When you contemporize, you make it very clear that you have specifically tailored your presentation to your present audience. You send the message that all your information is up-to-the-minute and highly relevant.

Contemporizing is favored by many entertainers, especially stand-up comedians. No monologue by Jay Leno or David Letterman is complete without an assortment of one-liners playing off the day's headlines.

But the technique is equally effective in business presentations. Did the stock market take a sudden nosedive or make a remarkable rally yesterday? Consider linking the news to an explanation of how your company offers its customers increased financial security. Did a local sports team win a major event last night? Consider referencing the event and drawing an analogy to the competitive environment in which your company is operating. In each case, be sure you make the current information link clearly to your main idea.

You can also contemporize right up to the minute. Refer often to prior speakers, to statements they made, to earlier questions from the audience, or to moments that occurred from the instant you entered the presentation environment: the conference room, the auditorium, the office, or even the building. Weave these references throughout your presentation at every opportunity. This technique is the zenith of contemporizing in its immediacy and potency. It is also the easiest to do. All it takes is concentration and memory, and it keeps you fresh every time.

Localize

Localizing involves referencing the venue of your presentation. As with contemporizing, it's a favorite among entertainers. Many rock concerts begin with a localized greeting like, "Hello, Philadelphia!," which never fails to draw an appreciative roar in response.

> 66 Refer often to prior speakers, to statements they made, to earlier questions from the audience, or to moments that occurred from the instant you entered the presentation environment.... 99

You can localize your presentation by finding facts about the venue that relate to your message. For example, you can talk about a particular client or customer of yours located in the same city and then go on to illustrate the benefits your company provided to that client.

You can cite an interesting fact about the city or state that supports your message: "Last year, over 500 patients in this city's hospitals died from drug interactions. Many of those deaths could have been prevented with our automated drug dispensing system."

Or you can refer to a noteworthy local person, landmark, or incident, drawing a connection to your offering:

> "It's good to be here in St. Louis, where one of America's favorite treats was invented almost 100 years ago. An ice cream vendor at the St. Louis World's Fair ran out of paper cups on a sweltering afternoon. Desperate for a way to keep serving his customers, he got together with the waffle vendor next door...and the ice cream cone was born. Today, we're presenting a new product that embodies the same kind of entrepreneurial creativity...."

Data

You can also create an external linkage by citing current data that links to and supports your persuasive message. The more up-to-the-minute and closely linked to your specific audience the data is, the better. If the data you mention is news to your audience, they will be impressed by the depth and currency of your information. If your audience members are already aware of the data, they will be quietly pleased that you are as knowledgeable as they are. Either way, you create a positive link.

To add a touch of emphasis, use the source of your data as a prop: "Have you seen today's *Wall Street Journal*?" (Hold it up.) "There's a striking graph on the front page that shows just how serious our industry's infrastructure problems have become." (Quote the most relevant number.) "This is exactly the issue our new system has been designed to address."

Customized Opening Graphic

The final and simplest type of external linkage is the customized opening graphic. Begin the visual portion of your presentation with a slide that shows the audience, the location, and the date of your presentation. I use such a slide at the start of every Power Presentations program.

A customized opening graphic might seem like a small item, but it has a powerful effect on both the presenter and the audience. For the presenter, it forces a final double-check to avoid the embarrassment of the wrong slide. It's also an up-front prompt that gives impetus to the style and content of the rest of the presentation.

For the audience, it sends the message that you've prepared this presentation especially for them; that it is not a canned recitation, but rather a custom-made work, tailored to their needs and interests. Thus, the slide launches the presentation with a fine stroke of audience advocacy, promising in effect that you are there to serve them.

> 66 A customized opening graphic might seem like a small item, but it has a powerful effect on both the presenter and the audience. 99

Roger McNamee, the co-founder of Integral Capital Partners and Silver Lake Partners, is one of the most influential investors in the technology sector and one of the best presenters I know. He is always in great demand to offer his unique views at major industry conferences. Roger carefully crafts each speech in advance and is keenly aware of the importance of customization. Here's how Roger puts it:

> Speaking engagements are great branding opportunities, but only if you do a good job. You can do enormous harm to yourself by not understanding the opportunity. It's a crime to give the "windup doll" speech, one that should be punishable by more than just not being invited back.
>
> If you don't feel some level of affinity for the community you are addressing, don't do it. If you do, you will only lessen the value of your brand. A speech is like a shark. It can't sit still; it either is building or destroying your brand.
>
> Personal brands have a life of their own, dependent on the perceptions of others. It's like cartoon characters who run off the edge of a cliff: They keep running in space until they realize there is nothing supporting them, at which point they plummet. A brand is the same: It's at the moment when everyone comes to believe that there is nothing supporting you that your brand collapses. Public perception is everything.
>
> It's death if you give a speech or a presentation that sounds like a prerecorded announcement. Odds are that you don't understand the critical success factors in your business well enough if you don't understand this truth.

Roger heeds his own advice by starting each speech from scratch, but his words are applicable to every iteration of every presentation.

Gathering Material for Customization

To customize your presentation, you need to arm yourself with useful information and materials. Customization is a process you should begin during your preparation period—days or even weeks before

> 66 Customization is a process you should begin during your preparation period…and continue right up until the moment you approach the front of the room. 99

the presentation—and continue right up until the moment you approach the front of the room. Here are some steps you can take.

Prior to Presentation Day

- **Research your audience**—Learn all you can about who will be attending: their knowledge level, key interests and concerns, and personal or professional biases.

- **Learn the names of some key audience members**—Know the names of several key influencers in the audience. Learn the names of the highest-ranking company officer, the most respected technical expert, and the manager with the most authority to make decisions.

- **Get current on industry news and trends**—During the run-up to your presentation, diligently search out news and media stories and Internet items related to the company and industry to which you'll be presenting.

On the Day of the Presentation

- **Customize your opening graphic**—Produce an initial slide that names the audience, venue, and date of your presentation and tee it up to launch your program. Microsoft PowerPoint has a specific function that changes the date automatically. (On the toolbar, select Insert, Date and Time, Update Automatically.)

- **Search for ways to contemporize your presentation**—When you awaken on the day of your presentation, watch the morning business channels on television, read the daily newspapers, and log on to the Internet; browse all these sources to find items relevant to your presentation and audience.

note

When you want to contemporize your presentation, consider these sources: The *New York Times* runs a daily feature called "This Date in Baseball" with memorable milestone events. Because competitive sports are an excellent metaphor for business, you could choose one of the events to analogize and illustrate your situation.

On a broader scale, several Web sites (such as www.historychannel.com/tdih/ and www.scopesys.com/today/) list significant events on any given date in history. On the day you present, find an event that parallels your story and incorporate it to add dimension to your presentation.

■ **Prior to your presentation, mingle with your audience**—Go out into your audience and chat with several individuals. Choose strangers as well as people you know. Ask them questions. Listen to their conversations. Gather valuable information as well as names and facts you can incorporate into your presentation.

> 66 Prior to your presentation, mingle with your audience. Go out into your audience and chat with several individuals. 99

CASE STUDY: KILLER CUSTOMIZATION AT CISCO

Don Listwin, now the CEO of Openwave, was for many years the executive vice president of Cisco. I first met Don when he was a junior product manager at Cisco. You'll recall from the Introduction that after Cisco's IPO, Cate Muther, the then-vice president of corporate marketing, required all her product managers to take my program. Don was in the first wave, and a diligent student was he. Before long, his advanced presentation skills earned him a plum assignment: He was chosen to announce the launch of a major new Cisco product alongside then-CEO John Morgridge.

This was a highly mission-critical task. Since its inception, Cisco had been engaged in a fierce competitive battle with Wellfleet for leadership of the router market. In 1992, Cisco produced a new integrated router that would strike directly at the heart of Wellfleet's strength—hardware—and exploit the vulnerable underbelly of Wellfleet's weakness—software—which happened to be Cisco's special strength.

Don crafted his presentation for the media using all the techniques he'd learned in my program and then spent the weekend before the scheduled Tuesday launch verbalizing in front of a mirror 40 times. On Monday, Don did a trial run in front of an internal Cisco audience and went into autopilot. His presentation had become dry and robotic.

He called me and said, "Jerry, I've gone stale! What do I do?"

I reminded Don about the customization techniques and he seized upon direct references and questions. The next day, just before his presentation, Don went into the audience and chatted with several people, asking them what they were hoping to hear from Cisco. Then he stepped up to the stage and began his presentation. Right after his opening gambit, Don looked at one of the people with whom he'd chatted and addressed him by name. The man smiled, and Don could feel the spark of recognition radiate through the crowd. (Later, Don likened this effect to what happens when a professor calls on a student, although I had never told him the story of Professor Drake.)

Then Don raised one of the questions someone had asked him during his schmooze, "Will Cisco continue to upgrade the performance of this new router?" Don promptly answered it

continues

by describing how Cisco planned to migrate the new product forward. Once again, Don could feel the energy from the audience, and it energized him in turn. He rolled forward with a full head of steam.

Less than a year later, Cisco's new router product was clearly the market leader. A year after that, Wellfleet disappeared in a merger.

Several years later, I was delivering my program to a group of new product managers at Cisco. When I got to customization, I referenced Don's example. One of the men in the group exclaimed, "Oh yes! I was with Wellfleet at the time, and I was in the audience for that prezo." He shook his head ruefully. "After I heard Don speak, I knew that the game was over."

Don still practices these techniques to this day to keep his presentations fresh and to connect with his audiences.

External Linkages in Action

Customizing your presentation is an art and, as with any art, it takes practice to perfect. Try your hand at customization the next time you present, and practice it every time you make a presentation in the future. The time you invest in making each presentation unique will pay handsome dividends in the form of greater audience involvement and many more priceless Aha!s.

The same techniques that make your presentation more timely, relevant, and compelling to your audience can also make preparing and delivering it more creative, spontaneous, and stimulating for you. The entire process serves as a feedback loop to invigorate you with the same kind of hustle Joe DiMaggio exhibited.

I practice what I preach. I've been delivering the same core material to my clients for 15 years. If I were to deliver it the same way every time, I'd be on full autopilot by now. Instead, I simply open the air vents of my mind, take in data about my audience, and then circulate it back to them. It makes them feel involved, and it makes me feel energized.

Although many of the external linkages require considerable but worthwhile prior effort, the most effective customization requires no preparation of all. It all takes place "live and in person" and is the ultimate form of audience advocacy: Concentrate on your audience during the presentation. This means weaving in many direct references to members of your audience and making many contemporizing references to moments that occurred since your presentation began. All it takes is concentration: Be in the moment.

> 66 The same techniques that make your presentation more timely, relevant, and compelling to your audience can also make preparing and delivering it more creative, spontaneous, and stimulating for you. 99

Of all the many presentation methods I've given my clients over the past 15 years, the customization techniques are implemented the least. Yet they provide potentially the biggest bang for the buck. They provide the most powerful ways to differentiate your presentations from the routine, impersonal, one-size-fits-all, plug-and-play presentations we see all too often. Learn these techniques and implement them the most.

> 66 ...the most effective customization requires no preparation of all...and is the ultimate form of audience advocacy: Concentrate on your audience during the presentation. 99

Professor Drake's lesson inspired me and has stayed with me all this time. Let it become the big bang for your buck.

THE ABSOLUTE MINIMUM

- Treat each and every iteration of every presentation as if no one in your audience has ever seen you present before.

- Customization is a process you should begin during your preparation period, days or even weeks before the presentation, and continue right up until the moment you approach the front of the room.

13

THE BIG TIME: PUTTING IT ALL TOGETHER

In Chapter 10, "Using Graphics to Help Your Story Flow," I described the symmetry linkage: starting your presentation with an anecdote or a data point and never mentioning that item again until your conclusion. The two references then serve as bookends. Once again, I'll practice what I preach: In the Introduction, I talked about my experience with Jeff Raikes of Microsoft. So, in the style of a Puccini opera or Broadway musical, let's reprise that anecdote.

It All Starts with Your Story

I spent an entire session working with Jeff to focus and organize his story and never once addressed his delivery skills. But that focus paid off. Jeff's presentation rang with conviction—not because of his vocal inflection, illustrative gestures, or eye contact, but because he'd gotten his story right.

> **"** A well-prepared story enhances a presenter's delivery skills. **"**

The lesson: A well-prepared story enhances a presenter's delivery skills.

Jeff Raikes's case in point applies to every presenter. Persuading your audience is, above all, a matter of being prepared with a logical, compelling, relevant, and well-articulated story. You need to know where you want to lead your audience—your Point B—and how you will get them there. To do that, you need to focus on the most essential elements of your story, arrange them in a lucid flow, and convey them with frequent emphasis on the specific benefits your audience will enjoy if they heed your call to action—the WIIFYs. Finally, you need to support your presentation with Less Is More graphics that express your ideas clearly. Your audience is then free to concentrate on you and your discussion: presenter focus.

If you prepare a presentation that includes all these elements at their optimum, a remarkable thing happens: Your speaking skills improve "by themselves." Knowing you are fully in command of your story inevitably enhances your self-confidence and poise, resulting in a far more polished and convincing presentation. That's the discipline by which most persuasive battles are won.

Are the specifics of the presenter's voice and body language important? Absolutely! Think of the diligently crafted story and graphics as a highly sophisticated communications satellite and the presenter as a powerful Atlas rocket. NASA spends millions of dollars and thousands of hours building such satellites. If the rocket (the delivery system) is defective, the satellite doesn't go into orbit. The same is true of the presentation. If the messenger is defective, the message goes awry. The well-designed substance needs an effective delivery style to lift the payload into orbit.

However, if I asked you to work on your delivery style before your story and graphics were "baked," it would be like asking you to rub your stomach and pat your head at the same time. For this reason, I have deliberately excluded delivery skills to emphasize the focus on mental clarity.

> **"** Persuading your audience is, above all, a matter of being prepared with a logical, compelling, relevant, and well-articulated story. **"**

There are a couple of other important reasons for this story focus. In the first place, businesspeople are not performers, nor are they receptive to being

treated as performers. If you were to focus on delivery skills up-front, you'd feel pressured to perform.
If, instead, you focus on the story first, you can
approach those skills in a natural and conversational manner.

This raises a subtle but rather potent point: When
most businesspeople stand to speak, they experience a sudden rush of performance anxiety. The
human body's instinctive reaction to anxiety is
increased adrenaline flow, which makes any possible natural behavior almost
impossible. Fight or flight follows. Clarity of mind diminishes performance anxiety
and allows the presenter to be conversational.

> 66 Knowing you are fully in
> command of your story
> inevitably enhances your self-
> confidence and poise, result-
> ing in a far more polished and
> convincing presentation. 99

Another reason for excluding delivery skills in this book has to do with how the presenter's behavior relates to the graphics. In cinema and television, armies of creative
and technical people spend extravagant amounts of time perfecting the synchronization of the images and soundtrack. The composite is then merged onto a single
screen, defining and confining the audience's point of view. In a presentation, the
viewing field—the audience's perspective—widens considerably from just the slides
on the screen to include the presenter's body language. The presenter's narration, an
entirely separate signal, serves as the soundtrack. Therefore, in a presentation, it
becomes even more important to synchronize all these diverse transmissions.

Unfortunately, all too often, the images on the presentation screen, the presenter's
body language, and the presenter's narration all run at vastly different rates of
speed. Slides designed in the Less-Is-More style free the presenter to do less and to say
even less about the graphics, allowing the presenter to concentrate on adding narrative value. This is further support for presenter focus.

Practice, Practice, Practice

Your sense of self-confidence and your ability to
persuade will be even further enhanced by devoting sufficient time to polishing and practicing your
presentation after you've done your basic preparation. This means verbalization, one of the essential
keys to making your presentation truly effective.
Simply put, the more time you allot to verbalization and its vital counterpart, spaced learning (the
opposite of cramming), the better your presentation
will be.

> 66 If you were to focus on
> delivery skills up-front, you'd
> feel pressured to perform. If,
> instead, you focus on the story
> first, you can approach those
> skills in a natural and conver-
> sational manner. 99

Spaced learning helps you take command of your presentation and makes you more confident when you deliver it. You will be less rushed and more poised. Spaced learning also helps you give your presentation greater polish. Each time you practice verbalization, you can find new ways to clarify your story. Finally, spaced learning gives you the time to make your presentation more succinct: to trim deadwood, eliminate interesting but irrelevant detail, and hone your fine points. The result will be a finely sharpened message.

Here's a checklist for your practice:

- Verbalize your presentation repeatedly. You can do this alone or into an audio tape recorder. You can also verbalize in front of a trial audience of colleagues or friends. In all cases, verbalize with your slides.

- Time your presentation to be certain that it works effectively within the allotted time period.

- Each time you present, use internal linkages to connect your ideas and external linkages to connect with your audience.

- Pay careful attention to your phraseology.

Make good presentation practices habitual, so that you employ them almost without thinking. Verbalization and spaced learning are enormously powerful tools that enhance the effectiveness of every other technique you've learned in these pages. Practice them!

note

A study cited in the *Book of Lists*, by David Wallechinsky, ranks speaking before a group as the highest anxiety-provoking event, topping fear of heights, insects, flying, and even death.

Every Audience, Every Time

I've demonstrated many of the concepts in this book with examples from my work with companies preparing for their IPO roadshows. Presenting an IPO roadshow is the ultimate in mission-critical assignments: It's like piloting a space shuttle flight, conducting the New York Philharmonic, or pitching the seventh game of the World Series. I hope you've found these IPO stories to be clear illustrations of the Power Presentations techniques.

66 Slides designed in the Less-Is-More style free the presenter to do less and to say even less about the graphics, allowing the presenter to concentrate on adding narrative value. 99

More importantly, I hope you've recognized that these very same techniques can and should be used in every persuasive situation. Their fundamentals have existed since Aristotle. The likes of Abraham Lincoln; Winston Churchill; John F. Kennedy; and Martin Luther King, Jr., all have used these fundamentals. You can use them, too.

> **66** Simply put, the more time you allot to verbalization and its vital counterpart, spaced learning (the opposite of cramming), the better your presentation will be. **99**

You might have a long and successful business career and never have the opportunity to present in an IPO roadshow. You might work in a field that isn't usually considered part of the business world: a government agency, a community organization, or a nonprofit group that provides many important and valuable services to our society. You might even work on a strictly unpaid, volunteer basis, perhaps as an officer of the Rotary club, the school board, or a charitable foundation.

No matter what kind of presentations you make, no matter where you make them, and no matter who your audiences are, you want to make your presentations as powerful and as persuasive as possible. The challenge is as urgent as convincing your company's executive team to support your new business idea, as close to home as winning your neighbor's support in a local election, or as personal as capturing the delighted interest of a classroom of first graders on Open School day. In every case, your results are on the line.

Video recorders make you self-conscious about the way you appear; audio-only recordings allow you to concentrate on your narrative.

If a presentation is worth doing at all, it's worth doing well. Be all that you can be. Invest the time and energy to make every presentation a Power Presentation.

You may never get to pitch in the seventh game of the World Series, but every time you set out to persuade, you're pitching in the majors. Go for the win!

The Absolute Minimum

- Knowing you are fully in command of your story inevitably enhances your self-confidence and poise, resulting in a far more polished and convincing presentation.
- The more time you allot to verbalization and its vital counterpart, spaced learning, the better your presentation will be.

PART V

APPENDIX

APPENDIX

TOOLS OF THE TRADE

Using the Storyboard Flow Form

The storyboard flow form combines the story form (from Chapter 6, "Starting Your Story: Capturing Your Audience Immediately") with a storyboard, relating all the previously mentioned techniques in one integrated view (see Figure A.1). By combining a well-constructed story that has a clear beginning, middle, and end with the slide layout, you can see how to express your entire presentation. This is the ultimate forest view.

FIGURE A.1

The storyboard
flow form.

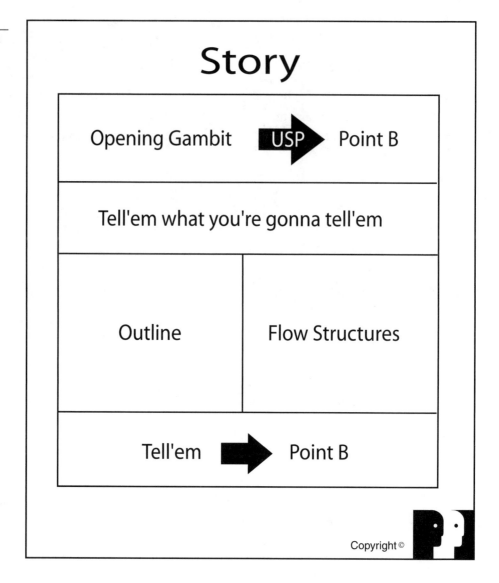

Make a photocopy of the form and fill it out for every presentation you create. The form provides a useful guide for putting all your essential elements together. Notice that I've left the slides blank. They contain only high-level concepts and dynamic inflection points so you can focus on the flow. Here's how it works:

The opening title slide is the background for the opening gambit, which links to…

The unique selling proposition (USP) slide, which links to…

The proof of concept slide, which is where the linkages culminate in a spoken Point B.

This is followed by the all-important (and often overlooked) forward link to the overview slide, which serves as a preview of the entire presentation. This is followed by another forward link to a statement that the overview serves as a roadmap, or an agenda, which is then followed by a forecast of the time. Then, you return to the top of the roadmap to begin the presentation.

The narration then navigates through all the slides in the full body of the presentation. In the example in Figure A.1, the Opportunity/Leverage Flow Structure organizes all the slides. Upon concluding the body, you move to…

The summary slide, which recapitulates the entire presentation and concludes in a spoken Point B.

Finally, the company logo slide leaves the audience with the brand image of your company, reinforcing your Point B (I see and I remember).

The storyboard flow form provides the 35,000-foot overview of your presentation, which in turn enables you to convey a clear sense of continuity and flow to your audience. When you feel in command of your material, you communicate a sense of confidence to your audience and heighten the persuasive power of your presentation.

The Presentation Environment

In the theater, the finest play by the finest playwright, from William Shakespeare to Arthur Miller, can be affected—for the good or for the bad—by the staging. So it is with a presentation. You could create an effective Power Presentation with a lucid story and vivid graphics that use every technique you learned in this book, only to have it all diminished by the presentation environment.

As the presenter, you bear the ultimate responsibility for your own presentation. To ensure that you and your graphics have the maximum impact on your audience, it's your job to optimize the environment. Here's a checklist:

- **Familiarization**—Arrive early and walk the entire presentation environment, not just the stage. Go to each part of the room and check the sight lines. Check, double-check, and triple-check everything.

- **Equipment**—Have a backup for each piece of technical equipment: computer, video, product demonstration, and projector. Remember Murphy's Law: "Anything that can go wrong will." Also remember its corollary, Sullivan's Law: "Murphy was an optimist."

- **Amplification**—Check the sound system and test the microphone. Most presenters need amplification with an audience of 50 or more. If you are soft-spoken, use a microphone with an audience of 25 or more.

- **Projection screen**—Present with the screen to your left as you face the audience. In the discussion of perception psychology in Chapter 6, you learned that audiences in western culture find it natural to move from left to right. With this arrangement, every time you click to a new slide, the audience travels from you to the screen and across the image easily and comfortably.

- **Lighting**—Keep the illumination low enough to create contrast on the screen, but never so dark that you lose eye contact with the members of your audience.

- **Pointers**—Lasers, retractable metal rods, lighted arrows, and saber-like wooden lances—all weapons—must be checked at the door. They are more hindrances than aids.

- **Timing**—Ask someone you know to sit in the audience during your presentation and send you countdown signals so you finish in your allotted time.

- **Liquids**—Drink water to moisten your mouth. Avoid milk and milk products because they coat the throat with a film. Avoid carbonated beverages.

- **Attire**—"When in Rome, do as the Romans do." Wear clothing appropriate to the event: suits for business occasions and casual dress for informal occasions. Men: Button your suit jackets. Women: Leave your clanging or glittering jewelry at home.

Unfortunately, the world is not perfect. The best hotel banquet salons; the most modern executive briefing centers; and even the slickest conference rooms equipped with the newest, most expensive, and highest-end equipment need to be fine-tuned. In the presentation world, the optimal is sometimes unattainable. If so, live with it.

If you overcome adversity, your audience will empathize with you, appreciate your effort, and value you more.

If the good Lord gives you a lemon, make lemonade!

Presentation Checklists

The Four Critical Questions

1. What is your Point B?
2. Who is your audience, and what is their WIIFY?
3. What are your Roman columns?
4. Why have you put the Roman columns in a particular order? In other words, which Flow Structure have you chosen?

WIIFY Triggers

1. "This is important to you because...." (The presenter fills in the blank.)
2. "What does this mean to you?" (The presenter explains.)
3. "Why am I telling you this?" (The presenter explains.)
4. "Who cares?" ("You should care, because....")
5. "So what?" ("Here's what....")
6. "And...?" ("Here's the WIIFY....")

Seven Classic Opening Gambits

1. **Question**—A question directed at the members of the audience.

2. **Factoid**—A striking statistic or little-known fact.

3. **Retrospective/Prospective**—A look backward or forward.

4. **Anecdote**—A short human interest story.

5. **Quotation**—An endorsement about your business from a respected source.

6. **Aphorism**—A familiar saying.

7. **Analogy**—A comparison between two seemingly unrelated items that helps illuminate a complex, arcane, or obscure topic.

Sixteen Flow Structures

1. **Modular**—A sequence of similar parts, units, or components in which the order of the units is interchangeable

2. **Chronological**—Organizes clusters of ideas along a timeline, reflecting events in the order in which they occurred or might occur

3. **Physical**—Organizes clusters of ideas according to their physical or geographical locations

4. **Spatial**—Organizes ideas conceptually, according to a physical metaphor or analogy, providing a spatial arrangement of your topics

5. **Problem/Solution**—Organizes the presentation around a problem and the solution offered by you or your company

6. **Issues/Actions**—Organizes the presentation around one or more issues and the actions you propose to address them

7. **Opportunity/Leverage**—Organizes the presentation around a business opportunity and the leverage you or your company will implement to take advantage of it

8. **Form/Function**—Organizes the presentation around a single central business concept, method, or technology, with multiple applications or functions emanating from that central core

9. **Features/Benefits**—Organizes the presentation around a series of your product or service features and the concrete benefits provided by those features

10. **Case Study**—A narrative recounting of how you or your company solved a particular problem or met the needs of a particular client, which in the telling, covers all the aspects of your business and its environment

11. **Argument/Fallacy**—Raises arguments against your own case and then rebuts them by pointing out the fallacies (or false beliefs) that underlie them

12. **Compare/Contrast**—Organizes the presentation around a series of comparisons that illustrates the differences between your company and other companies

13. **Matrix**—Uses a two-by-two or larger diagram to organize a complex set of concepts into an easy-to-digest, easy-to-follow, and easy-to-remember form

14. **Parallel Tracks**—Drills down into a series of related ideas, with an identical set of subsets for each idea

15. **Rhetorical Questions**—Asks, then answers, questions that are likely to be foremost in the minds of your audience

16. **Numerical**—Enumerates a series of loosely connected ideas, facts, or arguments

Twelve Internal Linkages

1. **Reference the Flow Structure**—Make repeated references to your primary Flow Structure as you track through your presentation.

2. **Logical transition**—Close your outbound subject; lead in to your inbound subject.

3. **Cross-Reference**—Make forward and backward references to other subjects in your presentation.

4. **Rhetorical question**—Pose a relevant question, and then provide the answer.

5. **Recurring theme**—Establish an example or a data point early in your presentation, and then make several references to it throughout your presentation.

6. **Symmetry**—Establish an example or a data point early in your presentation, and never mention it again until the end.

7. **Mantra**—Use a catch phrase or slogan repeatedly.

8. **Internal summary**—Pause at major transitions and recapitulate.

9. **Enumeration**—Present related concepts as a suite and count down through each of them.

10. **Do the math**—Put numeric information in perspective.

11. **Point B reinforcement**—Restate your call to action at several points throughout your presentation.

12. **Say your company name**—State your company, product, or service name often.

Seven External Linkages

1. **Direct reference**—Mention specifically, by name, one or more members of your audience.

2. **Mutual reference**—Make reference to a person, a company, or an organization related to both you and your audience.

3. **Ask questions**—Address a question directly to one or more members of your audience.

4. **Contemporize**—Make reference to what is happening today.

5. **Localize**—Make reference to the venue of your presentation.

6. **Data**—Make reference to current information that links to and supports your message.

7. **Customized opening graphic**—Start your presentation with a slide that includes your audience, the location, and the date.

Five Graphic Continuity Techniques

1. **Bumper slides**—Graphic dividers inserted between major sections of the presentation to serve as clean, quick, and simple transitions.

2. **Indexing/Color coding**—Uses a recurring object as an index, highlighted in different colors to map the different sections of a longer presentation.

3. **Icons**—Express relationships among ideas using recognizable symbolic representations.

4. **Anchor objects**—Create continuity with a recurring image that is an integral part of the illustration.

5. **Anticipation space**—Uses empty areas that are subsequently filled, setting up and then fulfilling subliminal expectations.

Index

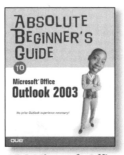
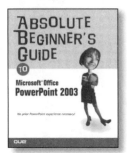